Synthetic Securities

by
Stephen Partridge-Hicks
and
Piers Hartland-Swann

Euromoney Publications Plc

Published by
Euromoney Publications PLC,
Nestor House, Playhouse Yard,
London EC4

ISBN 1 870031 86 5

Printed in England by
Bourne Offset Ltd., 2 The Ridgeway, Iver, Bucks. SL0 9HR

CONTENTS

INTRODUCTION

DEDICATION

To Bryce who taught us all we know,
to Lucinda and Dee for putting up with us
and to Richard for sleeping through it all.

18 September 1988
SP-H and PH-S

INTRODUCTION

This book is about synthetic securities; how to make synthetic financial instruments, and how to use them from the point of view of an investor. Throughout, we have tried to keep our exposition, of what is at times a complex and largely technical subject, simple and therefore readable by non-specialists. The book also attempts to cater for the demands of the expert audience by the use of footnotes.

The book has been edited, and mostly written, by Stephen Partridge-Hicks, vice president, Citicorp Investment Bank Limited and Piers Hartland-Swann, associate director, UBS Securities Limited, and therefore reflects our own viewpoints, and some may say, our prejudices. However, we have tried to keep our coverage of the market for synthetic securities as broad as posssible and to offer a text with the minimum of bias, or at least that presents both sides of a particular argument.

The book is structured in five sections and contains eleven chapters.

Section 1 (Chapter 1) reviews the factors which led to the development of the market for synthetic instruments and provides a brief history of its activity.

Section 2 examines the various components which can be used as the source instruments as well as the hedge or transformation techniques and examines the market trading and pricing conventions for each type. Section 2 comprises three chapters:

> Chapter 2 covers bonds, Chapter 3 interest rate swaps and Chapter 4 currency swaps.

Section 3 addresses the mechanics of making synthetic securities and looks at the effects on related markets. Section 3 is structured in four chapters:

> Chapter 5 covers three of the more usual ways in which synthetic securities and hedges can be combined or packaged, using as an example the synthetic US dollar floating rate note (FRN).
> Chapter 6 provides some examples of different types of synthetic security and explains how these can be created using each of the various hedge techniques which are currently available.
> Chapter 7 is a case study of the market for floating rate notes. It explains how investors became disillusioned as a result of innovations which were designed to benefit issuers, and how synthetic techniques can be used to satisfy investors.
> Chapter 8 examines the effects of the growth in synthetic securities on the bond and swap markets, and the implications of this for investors.

Section 4 covers the legal; tax and accounting issues and is in two chapters:

> Chapter 9 covers the legal structures used to evidence transactions in synthetic securities.
> Chapter 10 examines the tax and accounting implications for investors.

Section 5 (Chapter 11) provides a brief review of the major issues discussed, speculates on the future market for synthetic instruments and offers conclusions on the importance of this new market for issuers, investment bankers and, most importantly, for investors.

The book is representative of current market practice; inevitably it will become out of date as new ideas evolve. Nevertheless, many of the basic concepts and principles described in this book will continue to apply and we hope therefore that it will provide, at least, an introdution and basic primer to future investors and practitioners.

All errors and ommissions are ours. We will be pleased to receive any comments or corrections.

Stephen Partridge-Hicks   Piers Hartland-Swann

SECTION 1

The Market

Section 1 is about the creation of the market in synthetic securities.

It contains one chapter which reviews the environment prevailing when synthetic securities were first developed and explains the six principle factors which enabled their rapid growth.

In Chapter 1 we also examine the various risks which each investor must consider, and their balance against expected returns, when selecting alternative investment instruments. This section provides a framework for discussing risk management techniques in general, and concludes with an analysis of the specific needs, in terms of risk and return, of bank portfolios.

CHAPTER 1

Creation of the market in synthetic securities

Introduction

This book is about synthetic securities — what they are, how they are made, who buys them and why.

Before we embark on the main text we need a working definition of what a synthetic security is. Our definition is that:

> *Synthetic securities are hybrid investment instruments resulting from the combination of existing financial assets with hedge transactions, such as interest rate swaps, to create entirely new instruments.*

We shall return to this definition and expand upon it in Chapter 5 when the various types of synthetic security will be discussed in greater detail.

The market

The market for synthetic securities has evolved comparatively recently; by the middle of 1988 it was estimated that there were approximately US$ 50-60 billion synthetic securities outstanding. The authors made their first synthetic security as recently as mid-1985, and it is since about this time that the market for synthetic securities has experienced phenomenal growth. Yet, the principles and techniques have been both understood and available for some time. For example, one of the earliest synthetic securities, the gilt swap[1], was transacted in 1980 when an investment banker spotted an opportunity to make use of the newly developed currency swap when he discovered that there was investor demand for the resultant synthetic security.

Before launching into an explanation of the construction of these instruments, which we shall do in Chapters 5 and 6, it is worth first understanding the environment which prevailed in the mid 1980s so as to appreciate the factors which resulted in the rapid growth of this new market.

Factors for growth

A number of factors caused synthetic securities to grow into a discrete and significant part of the market in such a short space of time. These include:
— Development of the swaps market;
— Increased bank capital ratios;
— Global securitisation;
— Disintermediation of commercial banks from the capital raising process;
— Differential bank access to borrowers;
— Bank asset run-off.
These headings may appear to overemphasise the importance of banks. This is because banks in their capacity as investors clearly dominate the market for synthetic securities.

Development of the swaps market

The market in financial hedge transactions, in particular interest rate swaps, matured following a period of constant evolution during the early 1980s. By the mid 1980s the swaps market had reached a level of sophistication such that what had been considered complex transactions only a few months earlier were now becoming commonplace. Interest rate and currency swaps in the major currencies had evolved from matched counterparty transcations into an actively traded market made possible by the introduction of market making in swaps (or in swaps terminology *warehousing*).

In the matched counterparty swap transaction, to conclude a transaction an arranger had to locate two counterparties with equal and opposite needs as regards currency, interest rate basis, amortization and maturity (not to mention similar ideas on pricing). Swaps professionals soon developed techniques to

---

[1]Sterling denominated UK goverment debt (gilts) swapped into US dollars to produce a significantly higher yielding US dollar asset than US Treasury notes of comparable maturity, is described more fully in Chapter 5.

enable them to take a swap position onto their own books and hedge the risk of the differential cash flows by trading securities until the swap could be resold at a later date. The process of warehousing swap positions is equivalent to the use by a trading company of a warehouse in which all unsold inventory is held pending sale to a final buyer.

Warehousing reduced the transaction costs of individual swaps and gave swaps market makers a continuous presence in the swap market. This allowed them to execute transactions of much smaller size than they would previously have contemplated under the fully matched, counterparty, environment; they could now write swaps against existing swap inventory. The effects of warehousing resulted in an explosion of swaps volumes and consequently much broader application of swap techniques. This also made possible the development of the market in synthetic securities as a swaps warehouse is always open for business. Equally important, investors typically hold many small investments within an overall portfolio, none of which would previously have been swappable due to their small size. These small positions could now be restructured using the swaps market.

Increased bank capital ratios

The global trend towards higher bank capital ratios which was sparked off by the Latin American debt crisis resulted in banks becoming more selective about the use of their balance sheets to book and hold loan assets. These increased ratios forced banks either to increase the yield on their loan portfolios or attempt to generate income wihout the use of the balance sheet. The result was that banks adapted by making three changes to the way in which they ran their businesses:
— They started selling off, and not replacing, low margin loans to high credit quality borrowers. Instead, banks turned to lower quality borrowers so as to improve returns from lending. In doing this they took advantage of the fact that regulators do not distinguish between loan assets of different quality;
— Banks also increased the emphasis on off-balance sheet products which in the mid-1980s did not require an allocation of capital. Particularly attractive were those which required bankers' traditional credit skills, such as interest rate swaps and trade related products such as letters of credit. This strategy gave them a natural competitive advantage over their investment bank competitors;
— Finally, banks made strategic moves to develop their expertise in products which would service the funding needs of their traditional customer base without having to hold those assets on balance sheet.

Global securitisation

The process of securitisation had taken a firm grip of financial markets worldwide. What had started as a trickle in the late 1970s on Wall Street had turned into a flood. Every kind of financial asset was being restructured, repackaged and offered for sale. This was, in part, a reponse to the higher capital ratios discussed above, as bankers started to trade their asset portfolios so as to generate revenues without carrying assets on balance sheet. Banks in those countries that were most exposed to Latin American and other loan deficit countries found that they were facing higher reserve requirements than banks in other countries. This was because their regulators had reacted to the crisis by increasing capital ratios with the aim of strengthening bank liquidity and solvency. This resulted in a comparative advantage between banks from different regulatory environments which in turn created a new trade in financial assets.

Investors took to the new securitised world with considerable enthusiasm. They quickly learned the advantages of owning liquid assets which could be traded continuously, allowing them to adjust their portfolio risk and return profiles to changing market conditions. Both the volatility of financial markets, (most notably the gyrations of the US dollar which first soared, taking with it the US Treasury bond market, and then dived), but also the decline in interest rates worldwide helped to foster the move towards global securitisation.

Commercial bank disintermediation

As securitisation became more developed it started to be used as a technique to displace traditional sources of financing. For borrowers this meant substituting bank loans for issues of securities both in domestic markets and, more importantly, in the Euromarkets. By reaching providers of funds more directly by issuing securities, sovereign and corporate borrowers alike encroached upon banks' traditional sources of funds. Often, they were able to drive down their borrowing costs to similar, or in some cases lower, levels than banks who had previously lent to them.

This process of *disintermediation* was extremely active during the mid 1980s. For long-term debt this occurred through the issuance of instruments such as Eurobonds and floating rate notes. For short-term debt this took the form of Euro-commercial paper and Euronotes.

The result was that borrowers everywhere seized the opportunities presented by the new environment and established their own in-house banking departments, much to the dismay of bankers, who regarded competition from such sources as an unneccesary hardship in already difficult market conditions. The response of bankers was to rapidly develop their securities issuance, trading and distribution activities. This occured to such an extent that commercial banks, who only a few years previously had no Euromarket presence, soon had sales and trading operations to rival those of the traditional investment banks.

Differential bank access to borrowers

Some banks were successful in building securities trading activities and in generating revenues from this new business. Others, in particular those with low capital ratio requirements who perhaps found the need less pressing, responded less quickly. They soon found themselves without the products neccesary to sustain their traditional customer relationships in this newly securitised world. This resulted in *differential access* both to borrowers and therefore to transactions.

Although many banks were prepared to participate in transactions, they did not have the product skills or borrower contacts to originate deals themselves in a size they could hold for their own account. This led to a concentration of new issues origination among a small number of banks with strong trading capabilities. Most of these originators had no interest in holding paper on their own balance sheet and were active in distribution of securities to fixed income investors and bank portfolio managers. Those banks unable to orginate transactions became reliant upon sourcing assets for their portfolios from originating banks, fostering the trade in securitised assets discussed above.

Bank asset run-off

As bank loan portfolios started to run down, banks not surprisingly found that their traditional income stream was declining equally fast. The revenue stream from fee generating products and earnings from trading and positioning the new financial instruments were found to be of much lower quality, being both more risky and more volatile. (Interestingly, this is quite the opposite from the intentions of regulators, whose aim had been to improve the strength of the banking industry and make it more resilient to external shocks.)

Part of the problem in the variance of returns from these new activities was that commercial banks, in particular, had little experience of managing the risks inherent in trading securities. Even banks with better risk management experience did not make the transition from commercial lending to trading and distributing securities painlessly. Risk management tools for hedging trading positions either were not widely available, or had to be imported from other markets – such as the US Treasury bond market – and this often created new types of risk (such as basis risk[2]) where they were trying to reduce risk.

Summary

For all these reasons – development of the swaps market, increased bank capital ratios, securitisation, disintermediation, differential access to borrowers and bank asset run-off – the conditions were right for the development of a new market in financial assets. This market would use the recently developed swaps technology to create the type of high yielding assets that some banks would like to hold in portfolio but could not source themselves in the newly securitised environment.

[2]The risk arising from differences in the way that similar or related markets move.

Why buy synthetic instruments?

Before discussing how the new financial technology may be used to solve some of the many problems facing investors and bankers in the securitised environment, we must first review the risks and rewards which all investors expect when selecting investments for their portfolios.

Sources of investment instruments

Every investor must determine exactly the nature of the instruments he wants to hold and attempt to obtain them either directly from:
— issuers;
— indirectly in the secondary market for financial assets, or;
— using new financial technology, such as swaps, to create some combination of investment and swap which together have the investor's desired performance characteristics.

Risk considerations

The considerations for any investment, irrespective of its source, are broadly similar:
— Credit risk;
— Liquidity risk;
— Interest rate risk;
— Yield available on a risk adjusted basis.

Equally, these may be thought of as answers to the five questions:

1 What likelihood do I have of being repaid in full on the maturity date of my investment?
2 What risks do I face in funding the asset over time or in selling the asset in the secondary market before maturity?
3 What is the risk that the cost of funding the asset will change in relation to the return?
4 What is the risk that the realisable value of the asset will fall below the cost of the liabilities used to finance its purchase? (This is equivalent to question 3, but from the point of view of capital values rather than income.)
5 What return do I get for taking these risks?

As each of risks 1 to 4 increases, or is perceived as increasing, the return the investor expects in 5 will increase in proportion.

Other investment considerations

In addition, the investor may also have a number of subsidiary considerations. Each one of these, if not satisfactorily resolved, may be overriding. Therefore, the following conditions should be met if the investment selected is to be wholly satisfactory.

— Accounting for the investment should be straightforward;
— Settlement of the principal and payments of interest should require minimal administrative effort;
— Revaluation prices and sale prices must be readily available;
— Documentation evidencing ownership and control of the asset should be both effective and minimal;
— The investor's credit lines should be considerd a finite resource and not be used unnecessarily.

Risk analysis of investment instruments

Based on these considerations let us analyse the three key issues of credit risk, liquidity risk and interest rate risk, and attempt to relate them to the environment as discussed above.

Credit risk

Investors manage the credit risk or risk of default in their portfolios by using a number of techniques.

By owning a range of instruments of the same type, but issued by different borrowers, an investor can minimise his credit exposure to any individual or sub-group of borrowers. This principle of *pooling* or of avoiding concentrations of risk is one of the most simple and most effective ways of reducing default risk.

By diversifying into lower risk instruments an investor can reduce exposure to systematic changes in market liquidity or investor appetite for any particular form of financing. For example, an investor whose portfolio is concentrated in equities takes substantially more credit risk than an investor in money market instruments issued by the same corporation, since in default, equity is subordinate to debt.

By holding fewer long-term investments: these expose the investor to a much higher degree of credit risk, as he is committed to the borrower for the long term regardless of changes in the borrower's credit quality. Since the distant future is more uncertain than the near future, investors charge a premium for taking long term credit risk;

Credit risk can also be reduced by purchasing some form of *credit enhancement* for the underlying asset. All credit enhancement techniques offer the investor a second way of receiving the interest and principal amounts due in the event of borrower insolvency.

Credit enhancement usually takes the form of a bank guarantee in which the investor has recourse to the guarantor in the event that the borrower fails to meet any payments when due. This does not substitute the credit quality of the bank guarantor for the borrower of record, but adds the bank as a second source of repayment. This improves on the risk of lending to either the borrower or the bank separately. In many cases, the borrower would not have access to the market in the same form without a bank guarantee as the borrower's credit quality is significantly inferior to both the level typically demanded by investors and that of the bank. In these cases, the investor relies almost exclusively on the bank guarantee for repayment.

This is shown by the large number of Japanese corporate borrowers who came to the Euromarket between 1985 and 1988 by issuing equity warrants linked to low coupon bonds guaranteed by Japanese commercial banks. These borrowers were relatively unknown (outside Japan), yet they were able to place their bonds without much difficulty owing to investor acceptance of the bank guarantor.

An alternative method of enhancing a borrower's credit quality is the *first loss guarantee* in which the investor has additional recourse to a third party for a stated percentage of any losses. This is particularly popular with issues in which many different types of credit are linked together to pool risk as discussed above. This technique is usually used to improve the credit quality of assets which are individually too complex or too time consuming for the investor to assess, such as credit card or mortgage receivables. This concept has also been succesfully applied to finance-leased assets ranging from aircraft to motor cars. The investor is typically provided with information on historical loss records of similar assets and provided with a first loss guarantee for an amount up to these historic failure rates.

Liquidity risk

The risk that any investor takes when purchasing a long-term asset is that the funding which enabled the purchase of that asset might have to be repaid before maturity. There are three ways in which investors can manage this risk:

— by owning liquid instruments which can be sold easily in the secondary market;
— by matching the maturities of the funding and the assets;
— by controlling the net gap between the maturities of the assets and liabilities.

Many investors purchase investments with the intention of holding them to maturity. The most extreme example of this is the way in which banks used to run their loan portfolios. Loans were always held to maturity unless prepaid by the borrower. This was because there was no secondary market in loan assets as banks had no need to trade loans among themselves. However, many loan instruments now available have active, secondary markets in which banks can trade assets quickly and at low cost.

Some investors, such as life assurance companies and pension funds, have long term liabilities which are used to finance investments in long-term assets. These investors do not need liquid instruments for the same reasons as investors with short-term liabilities. They have no liquidity risk, due to the long tenor of their liabilities, but they may prefer liquid instruments which enable them actively to manage interest rate and credit risk.

Most investors, especially banks, who borrow to fund their portfolios are used to running liquidity gaps. By having longer term assets than liabilities they have risk on their continued ability to roll over their funding. These investors have developed sophisticated techniques for calculating their exposure to liquidity risk (such as measuring daily maximum and net cumulative outflow of funds) and actively manage this risk by extending the maturity of their liabilities whenever possible.

Interest rate risk

Banks are typically experienced at running loan portfolios matched by deposits either taken from customers or borrowed in the wholesale money market. These positions have little interest rate risk as long-term loans consist of a series of short-term interest rate fixings which can be matched by deposits with interest fixings of identical tenor. Banks are able to create gaps in their portfolios by funding at the very short end of the market (ie overnight) against loans with interest fixings of three or six months. In this way, they hope to profit from any positive slope of the yield curve, when the cost of the overnight funding will be less than the return on the loan. However, banks in general have little experience of fixed rate markets. This is largely due to the historic separation by law in many countries between lending institutions and the traders and underwriters of securities.

Institutional investors who benefit from having long-term liabilities such as pensions or life assurance policies use the same techniques as banks in holding longer term assets than liabilities and for the same reason: in order to obtain a higher yield from a positive sloping yield curve. Long-term assets have traditionally been fixed rate instruments issued by governments, municipalities or state agencies. Floating rate assets, however, are generally of shorter maturity and are usually held by banks. Institutional investors, because of the longer tenor of their assets, do not have a hold to maturity philosophy. The value of their investments is subject to large changes if interest rates change, and they need the flexibility to modify continually their exposure to this risk. Consequently these institutions, despite their small exposure to liquidity risk, nevertheless actively manage their portfolios because of their long-term interest rate risk.

Investors and risk

In summary, banks, and many non-bank financial institutions that have a banking function, are predominantly lenders whose credit evaluation expertise is focused on corporate borrowers. Their funding expertise is concentrated in the money markets. They use leverage of their small capital base to generate positive returns from small differences between their cost of funds and the rate earned on their loans. Long-term investors typically hold government, municipal or corporate paper which may be rated by external agencies. These investors do not focus on credit analysis in the same way that banks do. They trade long-term fixed rate securities and so their expertise is concentrated in the bond markets. Thus, banks are significantly different from institutional investors in the way in which they manage risk and generate a return.

Bank portfolio needs

Let us now review the specific requirements of bank portfolio managers to see how these have driven the development of the market in synthetic securities. We must contrast banks' needs with the types of instrument available in the prevailing environment.

Banks need:
— medium-term assets which are substitutes for the loans which they used to make either direct to borrowers or else through participations in syndicated financings;
— floating rate returns on these assets, allowing them to exploit traditional gapping skills;
— positive margins over their cost of floating rate funds (priced off the London intebank market);
— borrowers whose credit risk they are experienced at analysing.

Banks do not need:
— a high degree of liquidity in their asset portfolio due to their conservative interest rate exposure and hold to maturity approach;
— a 'mark to market' capability as they do not revalue their loan assets except in cases where the credit quality has deteriorated substantially;

However, the assets becoming available in the mid 1980s were:

— securitised instruments which were constantly revalued by the new markets;
— traded actively, if sometimes erraticaly, in the secondary market;
— offering rates of return which, if floating rate, were below their marginal cost of funds, or;
— if fixed rate, prevented them from using traditional sources of floating rate deposits without creating substantial interest rate risk.

Solution for bank portfolios

The solution was for investment banks to re-intermediate between the *supply* of recently issued fixed rate bonds and the *demand* by banks, and other money market investors, for floating rate assets. This was achieved by using swap techniques to change the fixed interest rate risk on new bonds being issued into floating rate risk.

These assets were designed to be particularly suitable to banks:

— by selecting bonds being issued by corporations (or other borrowers) well known to banks from their previous roles as direct providers of funds;
— by packaging the assets so that the short-term interest period maturity mismatch remained (providing the possibilty of a series of gapping profits);
— by providing the resulting instrument in such a way that it would not be an actively traded security (requiring the holder to perform daily revaluations) but would provide the investor with some liquidity to enable him to divest without undue cost if neccesary (although he intends to hold the asset through to maturity).

On this basis, a new market in restructured or synthetic securities was able to develop to solve the needs of banks and issuers alike. The next chapter will evaluate bonds, swaps and options on an equivalent basis. Succeeding chapters will show the process of combining swaps and bonds to create entirely new financial instruments.

SECTION 2

The Building Blocks

Section 2 covers the various component instruments and hedge techniques which can be combined to create synthetic securities. In this section we examine the market trading and pricing conventions of each of the types of investment instrument and hedge technique that are most commonly used to make synthetics.

Section 2 comprises three chapters:

Chapter 2 covers bonds, explains the various types found in the Euromarkets (including those which have aspects other than simple debt financing and are, in fact, bundled with other instruments), and concludes with a summary of bond valuation techniques, including the mathematics of maturity yield.

Chapter 3 is about interest rate swaps and explains what they are and how they are valued, starting with simple accrual accounting through the mark-to-market approach and ending with valuation on an implied zero coupon swap curve. We also discuss the effects of trading "off-market" swaps, the issue of reinvestment risk and the market forces influencing swap pricing.

Chapter 4 extends the discussion of swaps to the various types of currency swap technique. Again the focus is on explaining simple transactions, such as covered interest arbitrage, before moving on to more complex issues such as valuing currency swaps.

By the time that you have completed Section 2 you will be familiar with the most intimate details of most types of bond, interest rate swap and currency swap. From this base you are prepared for the various processes for combining bonds with swaps and creating synthetic securities. Readers who find the detailed mathematical analysis in Section 2 too exhaustive, or who only want to explore the concepts of making synthetic securities in Section 3, may want to skip the more advanced parts of Section 2 and return to them at a later date.

CHAPTER 2
Types of bond and valuation techniques

Definition of a bond

A bond is a securitised form of debt, that is, an obligation of the issuer of the bond (borrower) to pay the investor (lender) interest in the form of regular coupon payments and to repay at maturity the original sum lent. The coupon will usually either be constant (fixed rate), or vary according to some index (floating rate).

Before discussing bond valuation in detail, we must introduce a convention for illustrating the cash flows associated with any financial instrument. This will allow us to compare bonds, swaps and options on the same basis. The convention used throughout this book is designed to represent the magnitude and timing of cash flows of different instruments in a convenient and easily understood shorthand. An example is shown in Figure 2.1.

The convention uses a horizontal line to represent the passage of time, running from left to right. The left hand end represents the time when the instrument or transaction is created, and the right hand end the time when it matures. The vertical arrows leaving the line at intervals represent the cash flows over time associated with the instrument; an upward arrow indicates a cash inflow (positive) to the owner of the instrument, a downward arrow a cash outflow (negative), ie a payment that will be due from the owner. The position of an arrow on the line indicates the timing and its length is indicative of the size of the cash flow it represents. A series of arrows of equal height therefore represent fixed coupons whereas a series of variable height arrows is equivalent to floating rate coupons. Because of the big difference in size between principal and coupon cash flows with bonds and swaps we use arrows of different thickness to keep the diagrams to a reasonable scale: the thin arrows represent coupon or interest payments, and the thick arrows principal payments. Any cash flow that may or may not occur as a result of the exercise of an option is represented by a dotted line, to indicate the lack of certainty. All of these types of arrow are shown in Figure 2.1. The result is, of course, an entirely hypothetical instrument.

Figure 2.1: Example of cash flow convention

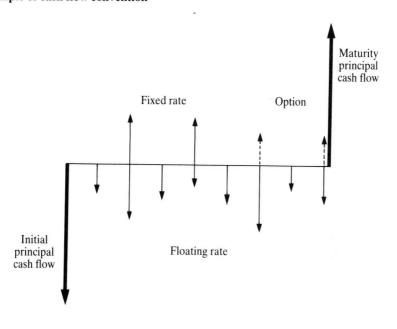

Types of Bond

Although bonds are, in principle, simple instruments, a number of variations are possible; many of these have been developed in the Euromarket and, indeed, are unique to it. As a result, we will refer in our examples throughout the rest of this chapter to specific Eurobond types because this is where the greatest variety occurs. However, the techniques will be equally applicable to bonds of similar type in domestic markets. Some of the commoner Eurobond variants are illustrated in Figures 2.2-2.7.

Figure 2.2: Fixed rate ('straight') bond

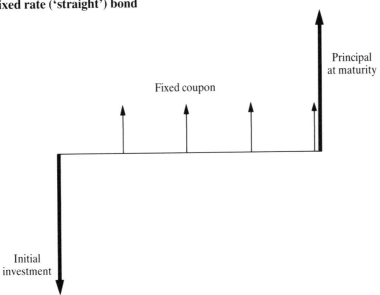

The initial principal cash flow is the purchase cost of the bond to the investor. Because the coupon is fixed rate, all the arrows are the same length. The redemption of the principal at maturity occurs at the same time as the final coupon payment, but in the interest of clarity, the arrows are shown side by side.

Figure 2.3: Floating rate note (FRN)

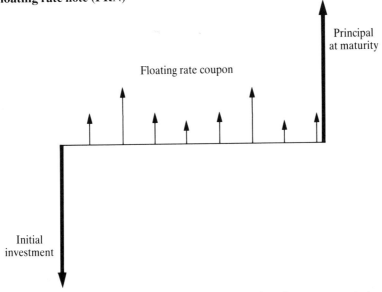

This diagram is identical to that for a straight bond except that the coupons, being floating rate, are represented by arrows of different height over time.

Figure 2.4: Zero coupon bond

Figure 2.5: Dual currency straight bond

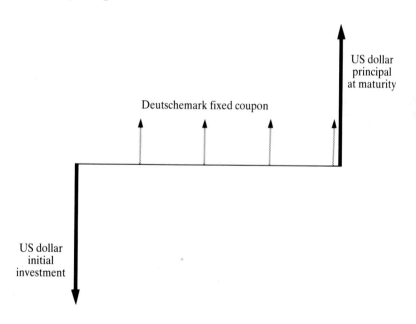

Here the coupon arrows (Deutschemarks) are shaded differently from the principal arrows (US dollars), to indicate the currency difference.

Embedded option bond

We have taken as our example a callable bond. The issuer has the option to call the bond on one of the coupon dates. The first figure shows the bond cashflows if the call is exercised, the second if the bond is allowed to run to maturity. The final figure shows how these are combined, by having broken principal arrows at both the call and maturity dates, and broken coupon arrows after the call date.

Figure 2.6 a: Call exercised

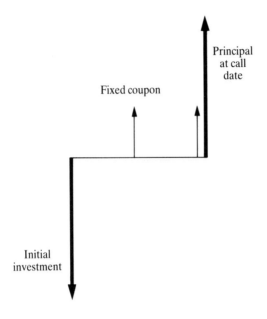

Principal
at call
date

Fixed coupon

Initial
investment

Figure 2.6 b: Call not exercised

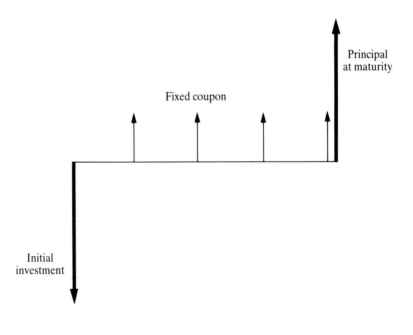

Principal
at maturity

Fixed coupon

Initial
investment

Figure 2.6 c: Callable bond

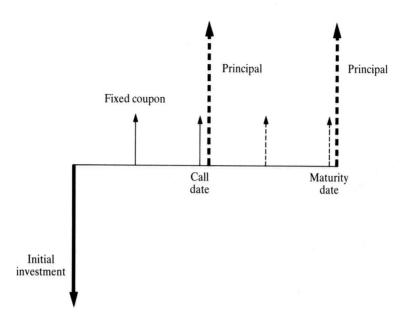

Variable Redemption Bonds

Examples of this type include 'heaven and hell' and currency linked bonds. The principal redemption has both a fixed element (shown by a solid principal arrow) and a variable element (the broken continuation of that arrow) determined by some market index or rate such as the Standard and Poors' 500 index or the gold price.

Figure 2.7: Variable Redemption Bond

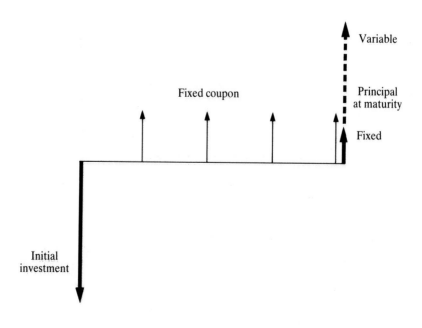

Bond valuation

The methods used in the markets for valuing a bond depend to a large extent upon the bond's characteristics. Nevertheless, all methods have in common the use of discounted cash flow techniques in one form or another.

Fixed rate bonds

The convention in the Euromarket is to value fixed rate bonds according to the following formula:

$$P = \frac{R}{(1+i)^{n+f}} + \frac{C}{i(1+i)^{f-1}} \left(1 - \frac{1}{(1+i)^{n+1}} \right) - C(1-f)$$

Where

- P Price, as a percentage of face value.
- R Redemption proceeds at maturity, as a percentage of face value.
- C Per period coupon, as a percentage of face value. (So a 10 per cent coupon paid semiannually would be input as a per period coupon of 5 per cent)
- i Maturity yield, per cent, per coupon period. (So an annual yield of 10 per cent would be input as its semiannual equivalent, 9.762 per cent, if the bond coupon were paid semiannually)
- n Number of whole coupon periods remaining to maturity. Any fractional period is accounted for the next term below.
- f Fractional number of coupon periods to the next coupon date.

Generally, all percentage terms (P, R, C and i) are input as their decimal equivalent, thus 1.00 for 100 per cent.

What this formula tells us is that if we buy a bond at a price P using funds borrowed (long term) at interest rate i, the maturity yield, then when the bond matures we will be able to pay off that borrowing in full, including interest compounded during the life of that borrowing. So, for example, with a bond paying a coupon of 10 per cent annually for 4 years, and an annual interest rate of 8 per cent, this formula yields a price of 106.62 per cent. That is, we can afford to pay 106.62 per cent of the bond's face value today based on a current five year borrowing cost of 8 per cent, and get paid out in full. What this formula does is to discount each cash flow from the bond (principal and coupon) at 8 per cent.

Using the symbols defined above, the long form would look like this:

$$P = \frac{C_1}{(1+i)^1} + \frac{C_2}{(1+i)^2} + \frac{C_3}{(1+i)^3} + \frac{C_4+R}{(1+i)^4}$$

or as the summation;

$$P = \frac{R}{(1+i)^4} + \sum_{n=1}^{n=4} \frac{C_n}{(1+i)^n}$$

The AIBD formula is simply the algebraic equivalent of this equation, modified to take account of a short first period (for valuing a bond in the middle of a coupon period) and any purchased accrued interest. It is Euromarket practice to buy bonds with interest accrued from the previous coupon date.

It is quite easy to plot the price-yield behaviour resulting from this formula to illustrate the inverse relationship between price and yield, and this is shown in Figure 2.8.

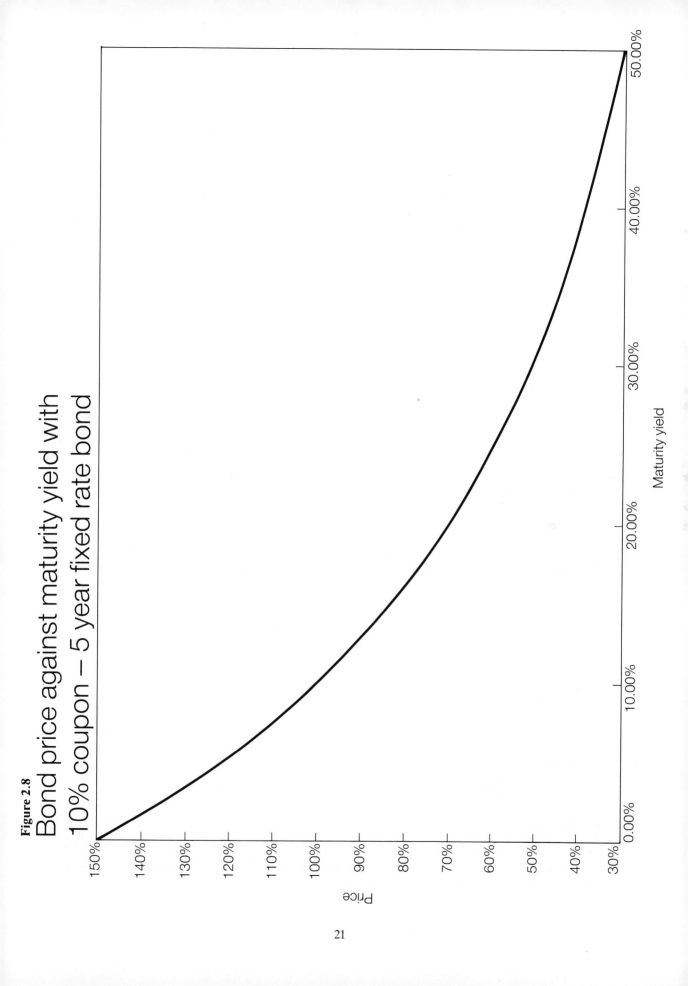

Figure 2.8
Bond price against maturity yield with
10% coupon – 5 year fixed rate bond

Price

Maturity yield

Floating rate notes

Floating rates notes (FRNs) are valued rather differently, using a concept known as 'discount yield' instead of yield to maturity. Discount yield is the marginal yield of the FRN over the index against which the FRN coupon is determined. This is almost always relative to Libor in the Euromarket, and the price against discount yield formula used by the market has the following form:

$$ z = \frac{1 + C + m\left(\dfrac{\theta - 1}{\theta\,(i + M)}\right) - \left(1 + \dfrac{fI}{\varnothing}\right)(P + A) + \dfrac{R - 1}{\theta}}{\dfrac{\theta - 1}{\theta\,(i + m)} + \dfrac{f}{\varnothing}\,(P + A)} $$

where $\theta = \left(1 + \dfrac{365.25}{y\varnothing}(i + m)\right)^n$

Where:

z Discount yield, per cent, per annum
C Coupon due at next coupon date, as a percentage of face value
M Quoted margin over/under Libor on the FRN, per cent, per annum
i Reinvestment rate, per cent, per annum (usually taken as Libor for the FRN coupon period, eg 3 months Libor for an FRN paying quarterly)
f Fractional number of coupon periods to the next coupon date
I Current Libor for the period to the next coupon date, per cent, per annum
$\varnothing$ Number of coupons per year
P Price, as a percentage of face value
A Accrued interest, as a percentage of face value
R Redemption proceeds at maturity, as a percentage of face value
Y Number of business days in year (eg 360 for US dollars, 365 for sterling)
n Number of whole coupon periods remaining to maturity

All percentage terms and Libor rates are input as their decimal equivalent, thus 0.0825 for 8.25 per cent

This formula is tells us that if we buy an FRN at price P using funds borrowed at Libor, then over the whole life of the FRN we will receive a total annual return (net of borrowing costs, assumed to be Libor) equal to the discount yield z. So for example, a five-year FRN with a Libor coupon, priced at 99.50 per cent of face value, will have a discount yield of 0.133 per cent. Buying the FRN at this price is equivalent to lending 100 per cent at a rate of Libor plus 0.133 per cent pa with Libor at 8 per cent; the discount yield formula simply converts the up-front price discount (or premium), and any extra return or loss arising from it, into its equivalent in yield terms.

One major difference from the AIBD formula is that the discount rate used to calculate discount yield is the current level of Libor; by using a short-term rate it takes no account of the greater uncertainty associated with cash flows further away in time. Also, the up-front premium or discount is not actually realised until the FRN matures, which makes it equivalent to a principal redemption. This is recognised in the AIBD method by using the long-term interest rate. Because the coupon on an FRN refixes every six months (usually) at a rate based on Libor there is little interest rate risk and so discount yield represents a credit margin that will change little with time. The up-front premium or discount will usually be quite small and the difference between using Libor or a long-term rate for discounting will be negligible. Since the formula assumes that the buyer has match-funded the FRN by borrowing at Libor, as most market participants actually do, it is really only safe to use it when the FRN has a price close to par and pays a coupon close to Libor. The effect of this valuation method on the market for FRNs, especially when the up-front discount becomes significant, is discussed further in Chapter 7.

Dual currency bonds

Despite the fact that the fixed coupons are paid in a different currency from the principal at maturity, it is quite straightforward to apply the AIBD formula to value a dual currency bond. For example, a US dollar/Deutschemark bond, with a face value and redemption in dollars and coupons paid in Deutschemarks would be valued in two steps. The dollar component is treated as a zero coupon bond, discounted at an appropriate dollar interest rate. The Deutschemark coupons are treated as a fixed rate annuity, discounted at Deutschemark rates and converted to dollars at the prevailing spot exchange rate. This gives a final dollar present value and hence price.

Bonds with embedded options

The commonest type of embedded option found in Eurobonds is one where the issuer has the option to redeem or 'call' the bond at some time before final maturity at a predetermined price. The buyer of such a bond has effectively sold a call option (or right to buy) to the issuer. The usual market practice is to value such bonds on a worst case basis.

If the option is 'in the money', that is, if interest rates were below the bond coupon rate on the call date, then the issuer would profit by calling the bonds. This would correspond to a bond trading at a premium to its face value. The coupon is higher than current market rates and the issuer would benefit by being able to call the issue and raise new debt with a lower coupon and hence, cost. The market assumes that this will be the case on the call date, and therefore values the bonds on the assumption that it will be called.

Similarly, if interest rates were above the coupon rate on the call date, the option would be 'out of the money'. The issuer would let the option expire unexercised rather than refinance the bond at a higher coupon rate. This would correspond to a bond trading at a discount to face value. The market assumes that because the coupon is below current interest rates the bond will not be called and so values it on a yield to maturity basis. Neither valuation method takes account of the 'time value' of the option that the investor has sold to the issuer.

Regardless of the current level of interest rates there is some likelihood that rates will change before the option can be exercised, or left to expire, which is not taken into account by using a worst case assumption. Whatever happens to interest rates, the call owner will always select the strategy that is most profitable to him and therefore least attractive to the investor. As a result, such bonds tend to be overvalued by investors. They have sold the call option too cheaply, being unaware of its true value.

CHAPTER 3

Interest rate swaps

An interest rate swap is simply an agreement between two counterparties to exchange streams of cash flows for a certain period of time. These cash flows are usually interest rate streams, and normally will be on different bases. The most common type of swap is one for fixed rate US dollars against floating rate US dollars. Swap maturities may be as short as one year to as long as 20 years but most activity occurs between two and ten years. Under two years there is usually little benefit to be gained from a swap, and beyond ten years the level of risk implied is too much for most players in the market.

In the US dollar market, there are two distinct maturity bands. Swaps for one to three years are quoted against (and hedged with) either Eurodollar futures or forward rate agreements (FRAs). Between three and ten years they are quoted in terms of yield spreads against the corresponding on-the-run US Treasury note issue. In other currency markets, interest rate swaps tend to be quoted in all-in yields terms. These quotation methods are a result of the way swaps are valued, and this forms the subject of this section.

Swap valuation

The basic approach to swap valuation is always to break down the transaction into the simplest possible components. The fixed rate side of a fixed-to-floating US dollar interest rate swap is easy enough to value. All the cash flows are known and can therefore be discounted using the maturity yield formula discussed above[1]. However, the floating rate payments, being determined by future Libor rate fixings, are unknown and therefore would seem to present some problems.

The way out is to consider a swap transaction as the simultaneous buying of a fixed rate and selling of a floating rate position. In the example in Figure 3.1, two counterparties A and B have entered into a four year swap where A is paying B 10 per cent pa fixed rate US dollars annually and B is paying A floating rate US dollars (ie Libor), semiannually. Both interest streams are calculated on the same US dollar notional principal amount, say US$1,000,000. Figure 3.1 shows how the coupon payments flow between A and B over the life of the swap.

Figure 3.1: US$ Interest rate swap

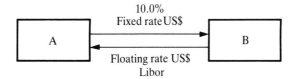

---

[1] The AIBD formula in Chapter 2.

In the form of an arrow diagram, B's side of the swap would look like this:

Figure 3.2: US$ Interest rate swap, B's position

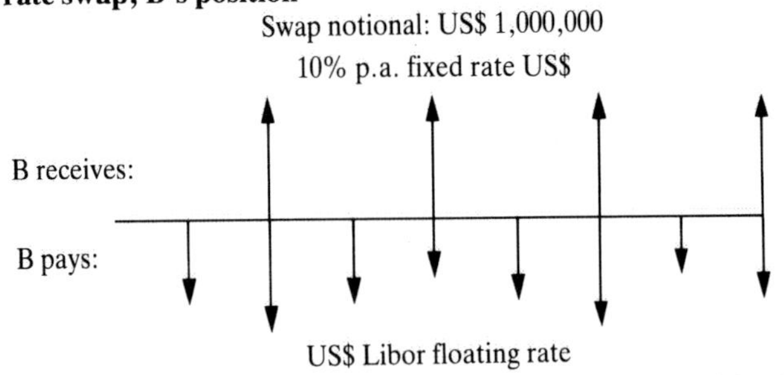

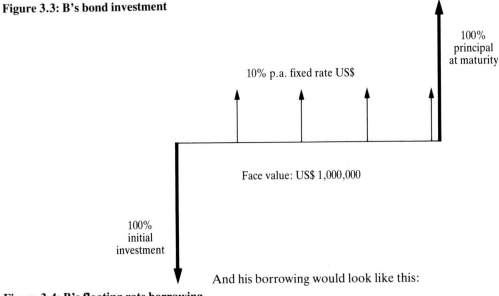

Swap notional: US$ 1,000,000

10% p.a. fixed rate US$

B receives:

B pays:

US$ Libor floating rate

B is receiving fixed rate and paying floating rate. If, instead, B were to buy US$ 1,000,000 of a four-year 10 per cent fixed rate bond at 100 per cent of face value and borrow US$ 1,000,000 in the money markets at a floating rate cost of Libor for four years, his bond investment would look like this:

Figure 3.3: B's bond investment

100%
principal
at maturity

10% p.a. fixed rate US$

Face value: US$ 1,000,000

100%
initial
investment

And his borrowing would look like this:

Figure 3.4: B's floating rate borrowing

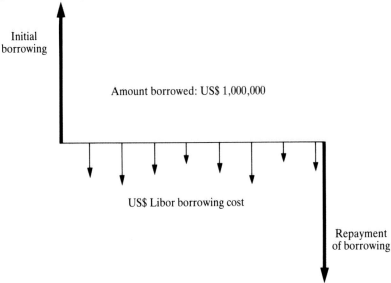

Initial
borrowing

Amount borrowed: US$ 1,000,000

US$ Libor borrowing cost

Repayment
of borrowing

Combining B's investment and borrowing gives us:

Figure 3.5: Synthetically created swap

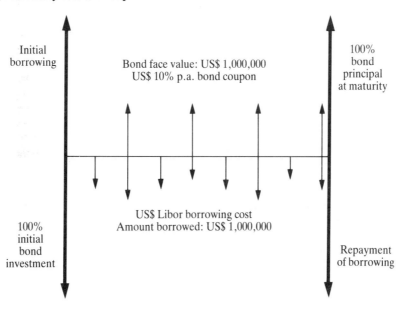

If we net out the principal arrows (since they cancel), what remains is the same as the original swap in Figure 3.2 above. The combined value of the bond and associated borrowing is nil. The US$ 1,000,000 borrowing cancels out the initial bond cost of US$ 1,000,000; the bond redemption at maturity of US$ 1,000,000 cancels out the repayment of the US$ 1,000,000 borrowed. The same amounts are being borrowed and lent, but on different bases, and since both are due in full at maturity, the two transactions must be economically equivalent. Therefore, the value of the fixed coupon stream must be equal and opposite to the value of the floating rate borrowing cost. Finally, it follows that because the fixed rate in the original swap is the same as the coupon of our bond in this example, the swap must have a value of nil.

We can see from this that a swap differs little from a simultaneous borrowing and lending of money on different rate bases. This is how the first interest rate swaps were created; as back-to-back loans. A major disadvantage with this method is its balance sheet impact. For example, a bank swapping a fixed rate asset into floating rate in this way ended up with double the assets on its balance sheet, double the credit risk, but frequently with a lower marginal return on assets. Quite soon it was realised that stripping out the initial and final principal movements had no economic effect on the transaction, and yielded substantial benefits. Credit risk was now confined to the interest rate obligations; the transaction could disappear from the balance sheet, and the marginal return on assets could be improved significantly. This use of notional instead of real principal cash flows was the single most important factor behind the explosive growth that followed in the interest rate swap market.

So far, we have only established that an interest rate swap has zero initial value[2]. We will now show that this is a special case and that generally a swap will have some monetary value during its life. Continuing the analogy of the fixed rate bond investment funded on a floating rate basis a little longer, what would happen if B were to unwind the bond position and repay his borrowing after only a short time? Let us assume that long-term interest rates have declined to 8 per cent. The bond, with its coupon of 10 per cent and life of four years is now worth 106.62 per cent in the market (using the AIBD formula). If B sells the bond and repays his borrowing out of the proceeds, he will realise a capital profit of 6.62 per cent from the transaction. The value of the floating rate borrowing will not have changed because it is floating rate. Since the bond coupon is 10 per cent and yields are now 8 per cent (that is, a bond with an 8 per cent coupon would be worth 100 per cent), this 6.62 per cent increase in value equates to the present value of the 2 per cent pa change in bond yield discounted back to today.

---

[2] Even this is true only if the swap is 'on-market', covered later in this chapter.

Before we go too far and say that swap rates are the same as bond yields (which they are not), we should return to our original swap and see how B would revalue his position when swap rates change. The basic method for revaluing a swap is to determine the cost of closing it out (unwinding it) at current market rates, essentially a mark-to-market approach. Assuming that the current market rate for a four year swap is now 8 per cent against Libor, for example, B's swap position and its unwind would look like this:

Figure 3.6a: B's original swap position

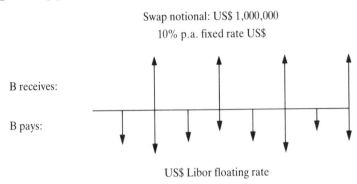

Swap notional: US$ 1,000,000

10% p.a. fixed rate US$

B receives:

B pays:

US$ Libor floating rate

Figure 3.6b: Close-out swap

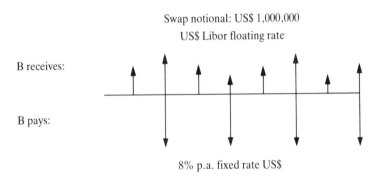

Swap notional: US$ 1,000,000

US$ Libor floating rate

B receives:

B pays:

8% p.a. fixed rate US$

Because the swap notionals are the same, the Libor payments, although unknown, will be equal and opposite and therefore cancel out. B is left with the fixed payments of 10 per cent coming in and 8 per cent going out. This gives a net 2 per cent pa profit for the remaining life of the two swaps in the form of a fixed rate annuity as follows:

Figure 3.7: B's residual swap position

2% p.a. fixed rate US$

B receives:

2 per cent pa for four years discounted at 8 per cent has a present value of 6.62 per cent. B's profit from a 2 per cent change in swap rates on a swap position is identical to a 2 per cent change in bond yields on a bond position. In other words, B's swap position, originally worth nothing has acquired an effective value of 6.62 per cent. This valuation method nets out all the unknown Libor cash flows associated with an interest rate swap, leaving only the known fixed rate ones. This is the reason why all US dollar interest rate swaps quotations use Libor as the floating rate benchmark against which the swap fixed rates is priced since this is how the swap is revalued.

Valuation: the market maker's perspective

Much of the development of the swap market has been strongly influenced by the accounting treatment of swaps[3]. From the point of view of swap market participants this has been driven by the need to recognise profit and manage risk.

Accrual accounting

In the early days of the swaps market, swap arrangers (usually banks) never took swap positions themselves but instead brought together a pair of counterparties for an arrangement fee. In time, they found it more profitable to stand in the middle themselves, replacing the arrangement fee with a skim from the swap cash flows over the life of the swap as in Figure 3.8.

Figure 3.8: Role of swap arranger

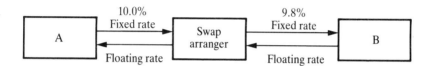

Here, the swap arranger has locked in an income stream of 0.20 per cent pa (shown below in Figure 3.9) by receiving fixed at 10.00 per cent pa and paying fixed at 9.80 per cent pa. The Libor cash flows are assumed to net out as usual. Accounting for such swaps, and recognising the profit from them, was easy since each coupon stream was accrued separately; the floating legs would cancel out, and the net accrual profit of 0.20 per cent pa could easily be recognised over the life of the swap in the accounts.

Figure 3.9: Residual retained by swap arranger

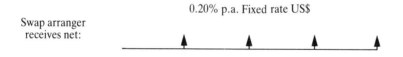

Mark-to-market accounting

Once swap arrangers started to take positions themselves, eliminating the need to have a pair of counterparties lined up simultaneously with equal and opposite swap requirements, it rapidly became clear that accrual accounting was inappropriate. It could not give any useful information about the true profit or loss associated with an open swap position. As a result, participants moved towards a trading approach when accounting for (and of course dealing in) swaps. Any open swap position (such as B's discussed below) would be revalued on a mark-to-market basis at its liquidation or close-out cost. This is, of course, analogous to treating a swap as if it were the result of a combined trading position in two marketable instruments. This cost could be expressed in terms of the annual cost or profit that would be locked in as a result of closing out such a position (for example the 2 per cent pa profit for B above). For the purpose of trading swaps, where there will be many such annual losses and gains in a portfolio, the present value of all of them is a much more useful number as it allows the dealer to model the effect on the whole portfolio of changes in swap rates.

---

[3] For a comprehensive discussion of swaps accounting practices see Chapter 10.

How swap rates are determined

There are several ways of explaining how swap rates are determined. As the pricing of a swap is not intuitively obvious, it is useful to review some of the most likely influences — credit equivalence, cost equivalence and supply and demand.

Credit equivalence

Since a swap rate is priced relative to Libor, which is a bank credit quality benchmark, it seems reasonable to suggest that the swap rate is the rate at which a bank would be prepared to borrow floating rate money and lend fixed rate to another bank.

Cost equivalence

Another point of view is that a swap rate is the best estimate among market professsionals of their expectation of the future average level of Libor over that period. This expectation should be adjusted for the value of known cash flows against the uncertainty of Libor based cash flows.

This view is corroborated by the way in which short-term swaps, with maturities under three years, are priced. Such swaps are hedged using various money market financial futures instruments. Typically, these would be US Treasury bill futures, Eurodollar futures, or forward rate agreements (FRAs), although the last two are the ones most commonly used in the swap market. Their most important characteristic is that they allow the buyer or seller to lock in a future interest rate today: thus a Eurodollar futures contract or FRA can be used to fix the level of three month Libor up to three years from today. This allows the floating rate side of a short-term swap to be hedged with a corresponding series of futures contracts or FRAs. The hedge rate for each Libor period is determined by the current futures price or FRA rate for that period. These hedge rates are then averaged into a single fixed rate for the whole swap, known as the 'futures strip'. It can be argued that a swap is effectively a long-term futures contract since it establishes the market price where one can hedge or fix a series of future Libors out to a given maturity.

Supply and demand

A major determinant of swap rates is supply and demand for fixed rate funds. Each debt market has unique preferences regarding borrower type and credit quality. For example, fixed rate investors tend to require higher credit quality than floating rate lenders. This allows different types of issuer to tap different markets for funding and then exchange the comparative advantage of their relatively lower costs. Issuers effect this exchange by using the swaps market in conjunction with their fund raising activities. Liability swaps by issuers have, until recently, been the principal determinant of swap pricing as they have been resposible for the bulk of supply. The development of synthetic instruments has created a new source of demand for swaps and has concurrently improved the efficiency of the swap market.

'On' and 'off' market swaps

A swap is said to be 'on-market' if the fixed rate side or 'leg' of the swap is executed at the then current market rate, while an 'off-market' swap is one where the fixed rate leg differs from the market. In other words, a swap is off-market if unwinding it in the market results in a difference between the swap and the unwind fixed rate cash flows. In the example earlier in this chapter, the initial swap between counterparties A and B was executed at the market rate and was now worth, as we have shown, the equivalent of 6.62 per cent up front. Effectively, it had become 'off market'.

It is clear that once swap positions start to be accounted for on a present value basis, it takes only a small step to start trading swaps with off-market coupons. Now, instead of B having to unwind his swap position with an on-market swap at a different swap rate, he can execute an off-market swap so as to match both the fixed and floating legs. In exchange for receiving a fixed rate 2 per cent above the market a swap market maker will be prepared to pay to B up front its 6.62 per cent present value equivalent (as in Figure 3.10a and 3.10b).

Figure 3.10a: B's original swap position

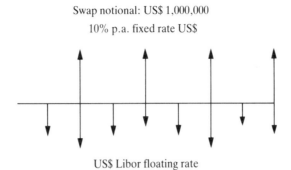

Swap notional: US$ 1,000,000

10% p.a. fixed rate US$

US$ Libor floating rate

Figure 3.10b: Off-market swap reversing Figure 3.10a:

Swap notional: US$ 1,000,000

US$ Libor floating rate

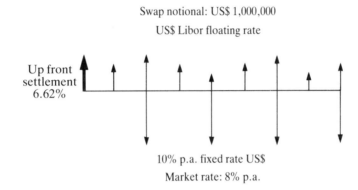

Up front
settlement
6.62%

10% p.a. fixed rate US$

Market rate: 8% p.a.

This was possible because swap market makers (that is, participants willing to quote prices for swaps and position them in advance of customer demand) saw benefits in matching all the future cash flow gaps in their swap portfolios, whether fixed or floating. It allowed them to realise the profits and losses implied by such gaps up front and reduce their interest rate risk. Any cash flow gap, being a fixed rate annuity stream, is sensitive to changes in interest rates. As a result, off-market swaps gained a very quick market acceptance and are now widely available.

So long as the AIBD formula is used to value swaps their price against yield behaviour and hence their revaluation will mirror the revaluation of a fixed rate bond. This is not really surprising since as shown above, a swap can be viewed as a synthetic instrument itself in the form of a combination of two bond positions. This is the theoretical justification for saying that if there were no basis risk between the bond and swap markets (when in fact there is), swaps would make perfect hedges for bond positions. The revaluation on a long bond position would be exactly offset by the revaluation on the matching short swap (ie paying fixed rate, receiving floating rate) position. Bond and swap yields do not move exactly in tandem in any market: the two instruments are used for different purposes by different groups of participants. As a result, changes in the level of supply and demand do not coincide, although there is usually a fairly moderate correlation between them. One factor pushing the two markets apart has been an increasing awareness in the swaps market of the inadequacies of the AIBD formula, particularly when it is used to value off-market swaps. This brings us to the subject of reinvestment risk.

Reinvestment risk

This is best explained by looking at an example from the point of view of a swap market maker trying to value an off-market swap. The trick is to see what gaps will be left when such a swap is hedged with an on-market swap and calculate their value. Figure 3.11(a) shows a four-year swap with a severely off-market coupon, along with the on-market swap (with the same notional principal) it will be hedged with, 3.11(b), and the resulting cash flow position 3.11(c).

Figure 3.11a: Initial off-market swap

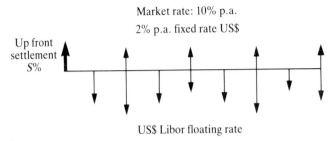

Market rate: 10% p.a.

2% p.a. fixed rate US$

Up front settlement S%

US$ Libor floating rate

Figure 3.11b: On-market swap hedge

US$ Libor floating rate

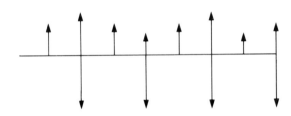

10% p.a. fixed rate US$

Market rate: 10% p.a.

Figure 3.11c: Resulting cash flow position

Up front settlement S%

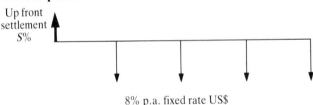

8% p.a. fixed rate US$

In this example, the problem for the swap market maker is to value the 8.0 per cent annuity shortfall out of the combined swap position. The smaller the up front payment he needs to compensate him for the shortfall, the more competitive his off-market swap will be. Using the AIBD formula with a yield of 10 per cent pa, the result is that S, the up front payment due to the market maker for the first swap is 25.36 per cent. So if the swap notional were US$10,000,000 (say), the up front cash settlement would be US$2,536,000. This cash will have to be reinvested in some way in order to meet the 8.0 per cent annuity shortfall, at a minimum yield of 10 per cent.

However, there is no real market for such annuities, and as a result swap market makers have been forced to try to find other ways to hedge the exposures these annuities represent, reflected in the way they value swaps. The most common ways of doing this use reinvestment rates determined by:

— The swap rate;
— The zero coupon yield curve;
— Money market financial futures instruments, such as Eurodollar futures as FRAs;
— Libor;
— US Treasury yields, or the relevant government security yields for the swap currency;
— The zero coupon US Treasury curve, derived from US Treaty strip yields;
— The implied zero coupon swap curve, derived from the swap curve for the relevant currency.

The annuity is determined with respect to the current market swap rate, and is then discounted using discount factors obtained from one or another of these reinvestment rate methods to determine its present value. We shall consider the relative merits of each of these methods in turn.

Swap rate

This method assumes that either another matching off-market swap can be done with an equal and opposite up-front settlement, or that an instrument can be found with cash flows that are equivalent to the annuity difference between the on-market and off-market swap, at a yield that will flatten the cash position. However, market makers periodically found it difficult to take the first way out because of market over-supply. The second way might be satisfied by writing an amortising fixed to floating swap against the annuity, except that there are few participants willing or even able to execute them for long-term swaps.

When market makers actually tried to hedge with something other than a swap they often found it difficult to achieve a satisfactory hedge (except in the case of short-term swaps, discussed below). If they were long-cash then they needed some asset yielding around the swap rate. These were very hard to find both in the size and quality required since historically swap yields have been well in excess of AAA corporate Eurobond yields, let alone government securities. If they were short cash then they could take advantage of the generally positive slope of the yield curve by borrowing on the short-term money markets at a lower cost than the income on the annuities.

Unfortunately, most swap books have tended to be long cash, especially in recent years. The explosion in activity in the synthetic securities market has largely been driven by the issuance of many bonds with very low coupons combined with equity warrants. This has meant that market makers have been receiving even more cash up front than usual (since most bonds are issued with coupons lower than the comparable swap yield).

Zero coupon yield curve

Another way of tackling the cash flow mismatch problem is to hedge each cash flow of the annuity on an individual basis using zero coupon securities. In the US dollar market the easiest to use are those (such as CATS) which have been produced by stripping US Treasury securities into coupon strips and principal strips. These trade as zero coupon bonds and a yield curve can easily be constructed. Each cash flow of the annuity is discounted at the yield of the corresponding strip in order to arrive at the value of the whole. This calculation, while tedious, is not unduly complex. The main reason why this method is not widely used is that although US Treasury strips are much more liquid than most other comparable zero coupon securities, they are still lack sufficient liquidity to be much use as part of an active hedging strategy.

Money market financial futures

Because short-term swaps are already priced and hedged off the futures strip, it is much easier to construct an accurate hedge for the annuity using the amortising swap method mentioned above. The reinvestment rate therefore simply corresponds to the weighted average futures or FRA strip rate for the principal amortisation of the annuity. Short-term interest rate swaps in currencies where there is no futures market use FRAs instead to generate the reinvestment rate.

Libor

In the example in Figure 3.11, using a Libor rate of 8 per cent to discount the 8 per cent annuity gives an up front value of 26.50 per cent, 1.14 per cent higher than using a swap rate of 10 per cent. This method gives the swap market maker some leeway in reinvesting the surplus cash from such a swap. However, it is not much used in the US dollar market, for two main reasons. First, any short-cash position being funded at Libor is highly exposed to an increase in interest rates since the yield on the annuity income has been locked in at a fixed rate. Second, there are better instruments available in the US dollar market for hedging these positions, as described below. However, in the foreign currency swap markets the choice is more limited and market makers therefore often use Libor to manage their reinvestment risk, combining it with management of their cash book.

Government securities

This method seeks to reduce the short-term against long-term yield curve gapping of the Libor reinvestment method by using government securities. At the same time, the credit quality of the hedge mechanism is improved, so it does not decrease interest rate risk at the cost of an increase in credit risk. Continuing the comparison of the example in Figure 3.11, above, a representative four-year US Treasury yield to use to discount the annuity would be somewhere between Libor and the swap rate, say 9 per cent. This gives a value of 25.92 per cent for the annuity. Unfortunately, the use of a four-year security to hedge a four-year annuity does not reduce the yield curve gap as much as might be hoped. A US Treasury note has a rather uneven cash flow profile compared with an annuity, with most of the cash produced at maturity. There would be cash shortfalls on each of the coupon dates, necessitating short-term borrowings on each fixed payment date, eventually redeemed at maturity out of the US Treasury principal, so there would still be exposure to short-term rates. As a result, this reinvestment calculation method is not much used.

Implied zero coupon swap curve

The ideal hedging method would combine the liquidity of the US Treasury market with the accurate cash flow matching of the zero coupon market. Theory would indicate that the yield on a given US Treasury note and the yield on the equivalent synthetic note created out of US Treasury strips would have to be identical. The fact that they are not reflects the greater illiquidity of the strip market and higher dealing costs that this implies. However, it leads to the idea that a security can simply be viewed as a composite of a number of zero coupon elements, each of different yield. This idea is discussed in more detail below, but the important point is that, given any yield curve, the zero coupon yields implied by that curve can be determined.

The basis of the hedging method is to start with the final cash flow and hedge it with an instrument of similar maturity. This hedge instrument has earlier cash flows associated with it and these are deducted from the corresponding annuity payments. The immediately preceding annuity cash flow (net of the first hedge) is also hedged with an instrument of corresponding maturity. This is done with each of the annuity cash flows in turn until they are all hedged. Using the implied zero coupon curve to discount the annuity stream gives a present value that represents much more accurately the cost of hedging.

Although it might seem paradoxical that it is the implied zero coupon *swap* curve that is most commonly used by swap market makers, there are good reasons why it is used in preference to the US Treasury curve. Computationally, this method is very complex but the benefits from using it mean that it has gained quick acceptance in the swaps markets, both in US dollars and foreign currencies.

Summary

With the exception of those methods using the swap rate (or zero coupon swap rate) or futures strip, all the methods used to calculate the present value of the annuity associated with an off-market swap assume that what is an off-balance sheet transaction will be hedged in part by some on-balance sheet items. Some thought must be given to the return that these transactions should be generating. Otherwise there will be a tendency for the balance sheet to become cluttered up with marginally profitable hedge items, eventually with adverse implications for such ratios as return on assets.

In summary, there is a complex series of trade-offs behind the choice of reinvestment method. Factors that must be taken into account include the liquidity of the proposed hedge instrument, its cost and credit quality, and the accuracy and management costs of the hedging strategy. In practice, swaps market makers use a combination of these techniques depending on the availablilty of instruments and their own particular circumstances.

Valuation: a more general approach

Hand in hand with the attempts of swap market participants to address reinvestment risk, there came a realisation that conventional methods of looking at yield did not provide a complete picture. As new instruments came to be linked or 'bundled' with swaps and as the methods discussed above came to be used to hedge swaps, it became clear that to analyse such problems a reductionist approach was required. This led to the thesis that all financial instruments could be broken down into combinations of just two simple elements, a cash flow, and an option on a cash flow, each of which can be valued independently. The value of the final instrument is then the sum of the values of its component parts. In order to realise this end we need some way to calculate the values of these elements.

Options

In the case of options much effort has been expended in recent years on developing arbitrage relationship valuation models, usually based on the work of Fisher Black and Myron Scholes. This has been seen most successfully in the traded options markets, where the divergence between theoretical and market valuations has steadily been reduced. The depth and efficiency of these markets has enabled participants to take advantage of the arbitrage relationships, allowing them to hedge options at low cost.

Some might argue that it is hardly surprising that the market and theory have converged when most participants are basing their pricing off fairly similar models. The main focus of attention in developing models has now shifted towards the kinds of long-term debt option such as those found in the Euromarkets. These tend to be long-dated calls or puts such as debt warrants and callable bonds, and puttable and retractible bonds. Such long-term bond options have proved much harder to value than short-term money market and currency options. Their price behaviour is a complex function of changes in the position and shape of the yield curve, affected also by the fact that bonds mature with a known value (usually par). This, combined with the illiquidity of the underlying bonds, makes hedging extremely risky and expensive. Also, when options are particularly out of the money (that is, when immediate exercise would be illogical as the option only has time value), they have no intrinsic value and the scope for error in determining their time value is large. Investors, who tend to be net sellers (or writers) of bond options, are now valuing them more accurately and increasingly demand proper compensation. This can be seen in the fact that callable bonds now trade at larger discounts to uncallable bonds than was the case a few years ago.

Single cash flow

Attempts to value individual cash flows have focused on the implied zero coupon yield curve approach. This says that the par yield curve (a curve composed of par priced coupon bearing securities of different maturities such as the US Treasury curve or the US dollar swap curve) gives a misleading picture of the true yields on cash flows. Under the par yield method, a four-year cash flow would be valued with reference to a four-year par yield. The problem with this is that the four-year yield is calculated from four annual coupons and a final redemption of principal (assuming we are talking about a Eurobond). This is really therefore a composite of the zero coupon yields of the individual cash flows.

Implied zero coupon yield curve

How does one go about breaking down the par yield curve into its zero coupon components? Essentially, the process is a recursive one, using the mathematical identity that the par yield of an instrument is a compound or function of all the zero coupon yields of the cash flows making up that instrument. To complete the definition we must assume that a par yield exists for each of these cash flows and that there is some point on the curve where par yield is equal to zero coupon yield.

Recasting what was stated above slightly more mathematically, we can say that for years 1 to n, the par yield in year n, i_n, is a function of all the corresponding zero coupon yields z, from z_1 to z_n, or in functional notation:

$$i_n = g(z_1, z_2, z_3, \ldots z_{n-2}, z_{n-1}, z_n)$$

or, by rearranging things a little, that zero coupon yield z_n is a function of i_n and the zero coupon yields z_1 to z_{n-1}:

$$z_n = f(i_n, z_1, z_2, z_3, \ldots z_{n-2}, z_{n-1},)$$

and similarly that the zero coupon yield for the previous coupon, z_{n-1}, is defined as:

$z_{n-1} = f(i_{n-1}, z_1, z_2, z_3, \ldots z_{n-3}, z_{n-2},)$

Eventually, by continuing this process of reduction we arrive at:

$z_2 = f(i_2, z_1)$

$z_1 = f(i_1)$

This is the point where zero coupon and par yield are equal since a one year Treasury bill is assumed here to pay its coupon at maturity. There are no intermediate cash flows so it is effectively a zero coupon instrument and the two yields are equal. We therefore have the starting point for the recursion and, given a par yield curve the solution process for all other maturities is then straightforward.

The following example illustrated in Figures 3.12-3.16 shows how this happens in practice. Here, we are trying to find the four-year implied zero coupon US Treaty yield. To simplify things we have assumed that US Treasury securities pay coupons annually so that there are only four zero coupon yields to find (whereas there would be eight in the real curve because US Treasuries pay semiannual coupons).

Initially, we have a four year Treasury, and we know the par yields i_1 to i_4 for years one to four. The corresponding zero coupon yields z_1 to z_4 are unknown.

Figure 3.12: Four year US Treasury note

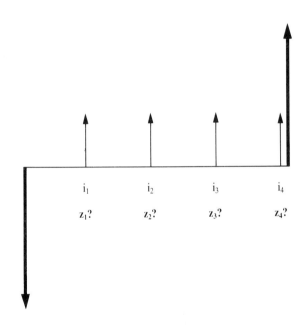

First we must solve for z_1, the one year zero coupon yield. We have shown above that this is the same as the one year par yield, so taking a one year US Treasury bill we have $z_1 = i_1$:

Figure 3.13: One year US Treasury bill

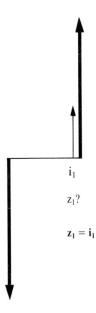

i_1

z_1?

$z_1 = i_1$

Moving to the two year par yield, since z_2 is a function of i_2 and z_1 which are now both known, we can solve for z_2:

Figure 3.14: Two year US Treasury note

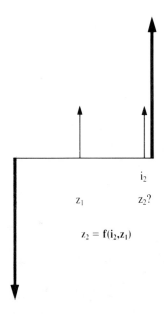

i_2

z_1 z_2?

$z_2 = f(i_2, z_1)$

Now we know z_2, we can solve for z_3 and z_4 in the same way:

Figure 3.15: Three year US Treasury note

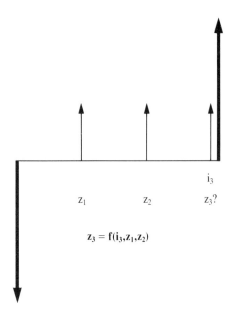

$$z_3 = f(i_3, z_1, z_2)$$

Figure 3.16: Four year US Treasury note

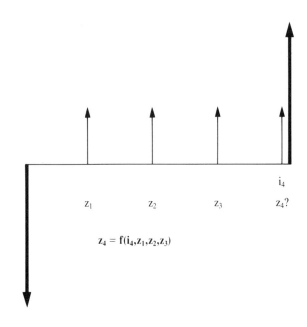

$$z_4 = f(i_4, z_1, z_2, z_3)$$

We have finally arrived at the four-year implied zero coupon yield by solving recursively all the earlier zero coupon yields that define it. This whole process is certainly much more complicated than using the par yield curve, and the above is a considerably simplified explanation of how the process actually works. Attempting to calculate a zero coupon curve by hand using even a yield calculator programmed with an AIBD type formula would be an extremely tedious undertaking, made worse by the fact that *any* subsequent change in the par yield curve will affect *all* succeeding zero coupon yields. Luckily, this process is fairly easily programmed into a computer, making the whole procedure not much more onerous than having to calculate the par yield curve.

Zero coupon yield curve

What are the benefits of this reductionist approach? Basically, it provides a consistent approach to valuing cash flows with respect to any desired market in a manner that allows that value to be realised. It considerably simplifies the valuation of a large portfolio of cash flows because it ignores the manner in which they have arisen. This makes it easy to hedge accurately the exposure to interest rate risk on a portfolio basis.

The main impact of the zero coupon yield curve approach on the swaps market has been a return to the use of swaps instead of Libor as a means of hedging gaps in a swap portfolio. Of more interest to the practitioner seeking to create synthetic securities, has been an increased availability of more complex swap structures (such as amortising swaps, or swaps with significantly delayed starts) which are considerably easier to value using this approach.

By combining option and zero coupon pricing techniques we can achieve greater precision in valuing complex structures such as puttable and callable swaps. By using the implied zero coupon swap curve we can determine the intrinsic value of any option and combine this with option models which determine the time value to arrive at the total value of the option. As these methods are applicable to both bonds and swaps we are beginning to see a convergence in the way that options on these instruments are valued. For example, a debt warrant with delayed exercise is simply a call option on a fixed rate income stream at some future date; this is not substantially different from owning a call on a swap (a 'swaption') with a similar fixed rate to the bond coupon, except in terms of balance sheet treatment. This approach thus permits hedging from one market into another on a consistent basis.

CHAPTER 4
Currency swaps

In Chapter 3 we have mostly concentrated on the US dollar interest rate swap market, although much of it is directly applicable to interest rate swaps in other currencies (for example, from fixed sterling to floating sterling). However, swaps from one currency into another make up a significant part of the total market for swaps. Currency swaps may appear to be more complicated than interest rate swaps, but we will show that they can be valued using exactly the same methods. First though, we will discuss some of the types of currency swap available, and how they have come about, before covering the main ways in which they are valued.

Types of currency swap

Although the simplest type of currency swap is considerably easier to describe than a standard interest rate swap, the combination of currencies and interest rates can frequently prove complex to value. Also, there may be several ways of getting from one rate basis and currency to another and it can often be very difficult to decide which method is preferable; as a general rule, anything that simplifies the process is to be preferred, but, as with all rules, there will be times when it does not apply.

Covered interest arbitrage

This is an old and popular swap technique first developed in the short-term money markets. Put simply, it involves the simultaneous spot and forward exchange of currency A for currency B at the spot and forward rates, as shown in Figure 4.1. Here, we have the purchase of currency B for currency A at a spot rate of 1.0000 and the simultaneous sale three months forward of currency B against A at a forward outright rate of 1.0100 A for B. The difference between the spot and forward rates is a function of the interest rate differential between the two currencies and in this case, since B is at a premium to A in the forward market, A is the higher interest rate currency (currency B is expected to appreciate relative to currency A).

Normally this type of transaction is used by foreign exchange dealers to take advantage of discrepancies between the swap rate (the forward points, the difference between spot and forward exchange rates) and the net accessible interest rate differential between the two currencies and thus make a risk free profit. However, as will be described in Chapter 5, it is a very suitable tool for hedging short-term money market type instruments (such as commercial paper) which pay no intermediate coupon into another currency. It may also be used with much longer maturities, through the long-term forward foreign exchange market, to hedge zero coupon securities.

Figure 4.1: Covered interest arbitrage

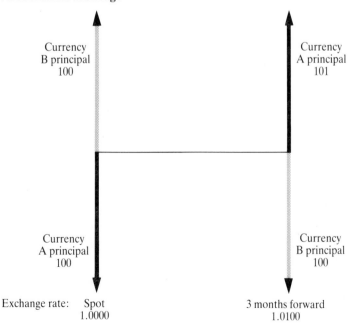

	Currency B principal 100		Currency A principal 101
	Currency A principal 100		Currency B principal 100
Exchange rate:	Spot 1.0000		3 months forward 1.0100

Long-term forward foreign exchange swap

If we want to receive a known constant fixed rate in currency B in return for its equivalent in currency A, with principals exchanged up front and at maturity, then the simplest way to do that, so long as we are not too concerned about how smooth the currency A cash flows are, is to use a long-term forward foreign exchange swap of the form illustrated in Figure 4.2. The swap points used to determine the forward outright foreign exchange rate reflect the difference in interest rates between the two currencies being swapped. The further out we go the longer the interest rate differential has to act and so the larger are the swap points. This can be seen in the way that the forward outright rate applicable to the coupons gets steadily further away from the spot rate, being furthest at maturity[1]. As a result, although we are buying a string of constant 5 per cent currency B coupons forward, the amounts of currency A required to buy them will be different, and so will not be a constant percentage of the final currency A principal paid at maturity. This makes it difficult to use the AIBD formula (which assumes constant coupons) to calculate the yield of the currency A cash flows but a more general form of the formula will still apply and so the yield *can* be calculated.

Figure 4.2: Long-term foward foreign exchange swap

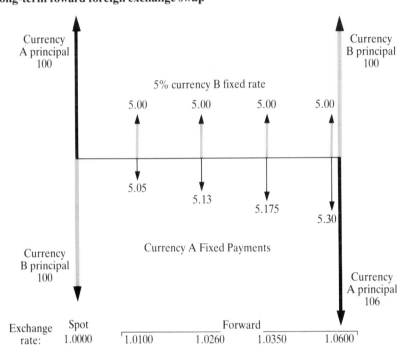

Because of the irregular cash flows that result in the target currency, this type of swap is not as popular as some of the others described below. However, when all else fails it is sometimes the only practicable way. It is normally possible to arrange for the irregularities in the cash flows to be smoothed out to produce a constant coupon. This will usually add to the cost of the swap (by reducing the yield in the target currency) and is rarely a worthwhile exercise. The use of long-term foreign exchange swaps by synthetic securities practitioners is well established[2].

---

[1] This will not always be true. The trend of the swap points depends on the relative shapes of the yield curves in the two currencies.

[2] See the section on Gilt swaps in Chapter 5 for an application of long term foreign exchange swaps.

Floating to floating currency swaps

This type of swap does not make explicit use of the long-term foreign exchange markets. Instead, it works on the principal that Libor in one currency should be worth exactly as much as Libor in another currency, all other things being equal. Figure 4.3 below shows a floating to floating swap between currencies A and B, paying currency A Libor and receiving currency B Libor:

Figure 4.3: Floating to floating currency swap

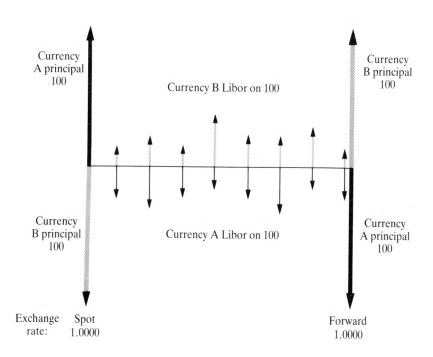

The most obvious thing about this swap is that the exchanges of principal spot and at maturity both take place at the spot exchange rate of 1.0000. This is known as a 'par-forward' exchange of principals and is an integral feature of this type of swap. The par-forward works because the transaction as a whole decouples from the foreign exchange market. The floating rates are determined independently in the two currencies, with currency A Libor calculated on the currency A principal and currency B Libor on the currency B principal. The exchange rates implied by the exchanges of floating rate cash flows over the life of the swap are a function both of the original spot rate and the relative level of Libor in the two currencies, but initially are unknown.

This swap is identical to a pair of back-to-back floating rate loans and the example above could be closed out using just such a technique. If we assume that the currency A principal proceeds of the swap described above are immediately placed on deposit at Libor and that the currency B sold into the swap is borrowed at a cost of Libor, both for the same period as the swap, then we will get the result shown in Figure 4.4 below for the borrowing, loan, and combined position.

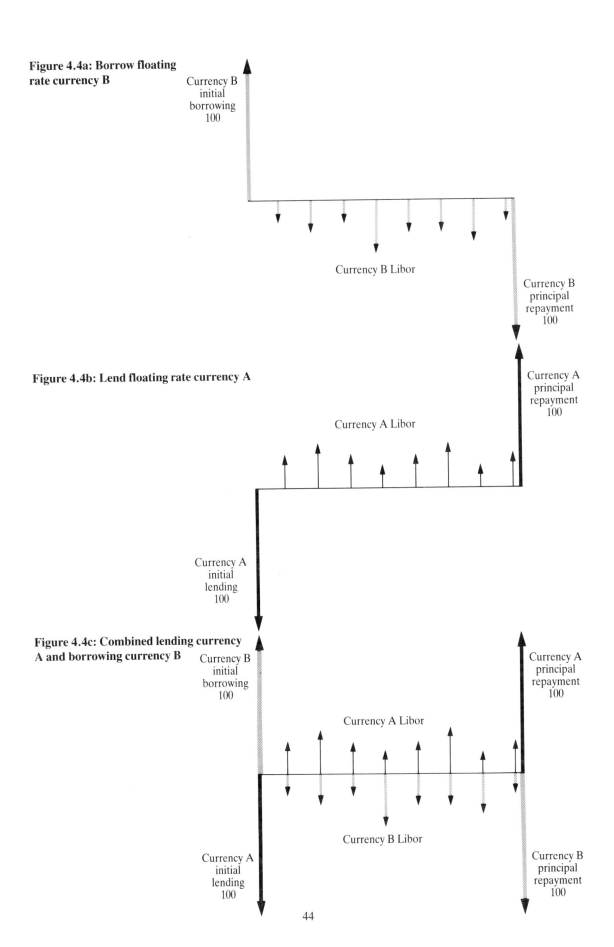

Figure 4.4a: Borrow floating rate currency B

Currency B initial borrowing 100

Currency B Libor

Currency B principal repayment 100

Figure 4.4b: Lend floating rate currency A

Currency A principal repayment 100

Currency A Libor

Currency A initial lending 100

Figure 4.4c: Combined lending currency A and borrowing currency B

Currency B initial borrowing 100

Currency A principal repayment 100

Currency A Libor

Currency A initial lending 100

Currency B Libor

Currency B principal repayment 100

It is evident that the combined borrowing and lending of Figure 4.4 produces a mirror image of the swap of Figure 4.3. Interestingly, this will be true whatever par-forward rate is used for the swap, so long as *both* the spot and forward exchanges occur at that rate. The swap position does not in itself create any currency exposure and there can be no exposure to long-term interest rates since both legs are floating rate.

Fixed to floating currency swaps

This is the predominant type in the currency swap market and is the most widely quoted. Typically, the benchmark for the swap rate is US dollar Libor mainly because it is the most liquid currency and also because most foreign exchange is traded in similar fashion. Usually the currency swap yield will not differ substantially from the pure interest rate swap yield in that currency (given that floating in one currency is equivalent to floating in another, as shown above), except where the local currency regulatory environment has distorted the relationship or where there is an excessive disequilibrium between supply and demand on the floating to floating swap.

Figure 4.5 shows a typical swap, receiving fixed rate currency A and paying floating rate US dollars. To create this swap we would execute a par-forward exchange of principals, selling currency A spot against US dollars and buying it forward against US dollars, both at the spot rate of 1.5000 A to the US dollar. Additionally, over the life of the swap we would pay US dollar Libor on the US dollar principal and receive the swap fixed rate, 10 per cent , on the currency A principal.

Figure 4.5: Currency and interest rate swap

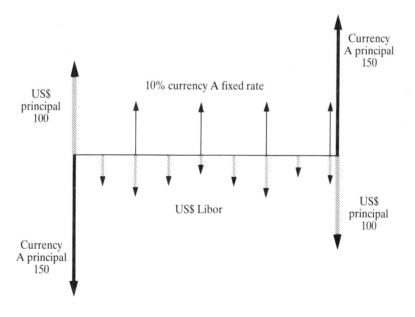

We can demonstrate that this swap has nil value initially if executed at a market rate by considering the equivalent two stage swap transaction illustrated in Figure 4.6 below. First, we would execute an on-market interest rate swap in currency A, paying Libor and receiving 10 per cent fixed rate on a swap notional of A 150. The second step is to execute a floating to floating swap between currency A and US dollars, selling the currency A principal spot against dollars and buying it forward at a spot rate for the par-forward of 1.5000, and receiving Libor on the A principal in exchange for Libor on the dollar principal. When these two swaps are combined, what results is a fixed currency A to floating US dollars currency swap identical to the one in Figure 4.5 above. Since the two components have nil initial value, so too must the sum of them. This example also demonstrates why the currency swap yield should not differ from the interest rate swap yield; the market rate came from the currency A interest rate swap and was not changed by the subsequent floating to floating currency swap.

Figure 4.6a: Fixed to floating interest rate swap in currency A

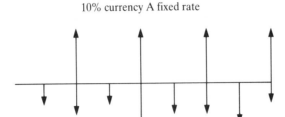

Swap notional: A 150
10% currency A fixed rate

Currency A Libor

Figure 4.6b: Floating currency A to floating US dollary currency swap

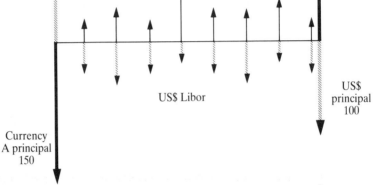

Currency
A principal
150

US$
principal
100

Currency A Libor

US$
principal
100

US$ Libor

Currency
A principal
150

Figure 4.6c: Resultant fixed currency A to floating US dollar currency swap

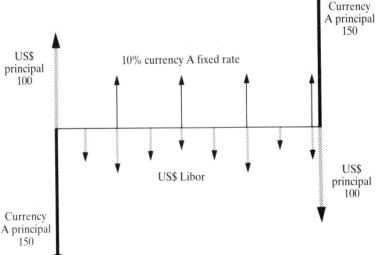

Currency
A principal
150

US$
principal
100

10% currency A fixed rate

US$
principal
100

US$ Libor

Currency
A principal
150

Whether one calls this type of swap fixed to floating or floating to fixed is a matter of opinion; the discussion above applies equally if all the cash flows are reversed. There is certainly no agreement among swap professionals as to whether the expression 'fixed to floating' means paying fixed and receiving floating or the reverse. Consequently, prudence dictates that when executing a swap one should always state explicitly what is being paid and received, and by whom.

Fixed to fixed currency swap

Rather than use the long-term forward foreign exchange market and then smooth the cash flows in one or other of the currencies, a commoner way of creating this type of swap is to execute first a swap into US dollar Libor (which may be an interest rate or currency swap if the source is fixed rate US dollars or another currency respectively) and simultaneously a currency swap from US dollar Libor into the desired fixed rate currency (omitting the currency element if fixed rate US dollars). There will thus be at least one fixed to floating currency swap, and there may well be two of them.

Figure 4.7 below shows the latter case with a swap from fixed rate currency B into fixed rate currency A resulting from a pair of swaps against floating US dollars. In the first swap we pay 5 per cent fixed rate currency B in return for receiving US dollar Libor on the spot US dollar equivalent of the currency B principal. As a result of the par-forward exchange, we are long currency B and short US dollars spot. In the second swap we close out the short US dollar exchange position by selling currency A for US dollars in the par-forward exchange, and pay US dollar Libor in exchange for 10 per cent fixed rate currency A. As a result, the spot and forward US dollar principal positions cancel out, as do the Libor payments, leaving us with fixed rate cash flows in currencies A and B only.

Figure 4.7a: Fixed currency B to floating US dollar swap

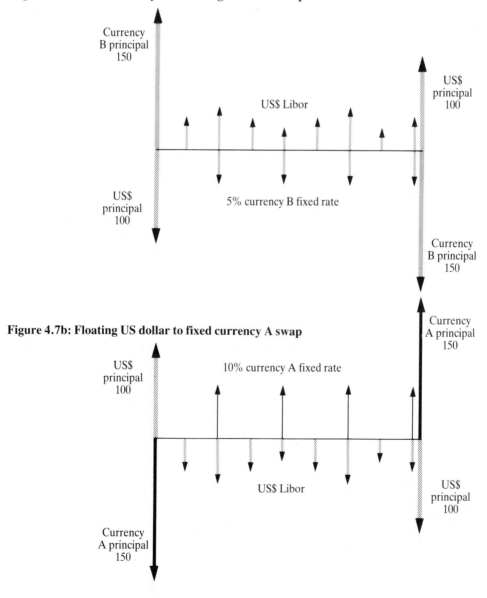

Figure 4.7b: Floating US dollar to fixed currency A swap

Figure 4.7c: Resulting fixed currency B to fixed currency A swap

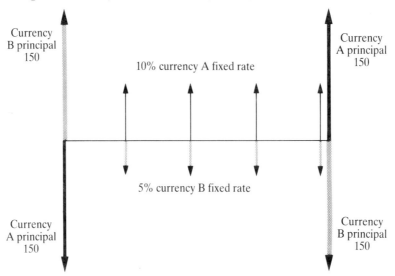

Again, since both of the fixed to floating swaps making up this transaction have nil value initially if executed at market rates, their sum will also have nil initial value.

It is clear that a fixed to fixed swap executed in this manner must have exactly the same value as the comparable long-term foreign exchange swap. Otherwise it would be possible to generate a risk-free arbitrage profit by creating a swap position by one route and closing it out simultaneously by the other route and pocketing the difference. Rather in the way that short-term (up to one year) forward foreign exchange rates reflect the interest rate differential between Libor rates in the corresponding currencies, so long-term foreign exchange rates reflect the interest rate differential between long-term interest rate swap rates. Because of this, it is not uncommon for banks in this market to have their long-term forward foreign exchange operations and their currency swap operations in the same department.

If both of the swaps are done with the same counterparty then the usual practice is to leave out the US dollar cash flows altogether and execute only the swap with a par-forward exchange at the cross-rate between the two currencies. However, the swap provider will probably view the transaction internally as a pair of swaps against US dollars since he will be managing the two currency books independently. Our ability to create this swap out of two fixed to floating swaps means that it is possible to shop around for the best rate in the two currencies; it is unlikely that the same counterparty will have the best rates in the market for *both* legs. Set against this, there will be a doubling of the credit risk (and, if reserve requirements for swaps are applicable, a doubling of the capital allocation) since there will be two counterparties rather than just one.

All the swaps discussed above have involved an initial exchange of principals at the prevailing spot rate. So long as the swap is being transacted at an on-market exchange rate this exchange is not strictly necessary as part of our swap with a swap market marker, since he can perform exactly the same transaction instead with another counterparty in the spot foreign exchange market. This is known as a par-forward swap without initial exchange. The majority of currency swaps used to hedge assets as part of creating a synthetic instrument will have an initial exchange, as described in Chapter 5, so this type of swap is not usually relevant.

Currency swap valuation

All the currency swaps described above will have a nil initial value if executed at a market rate. Thereafter, their value will change according to changes in interest rates and foreign exchange rates as they become progressively off-market. Since this revaluation process is identical to the procedures needed to value off-market currency swaps, we shall cover them both by describing the valuation methods for different off-market situations, some of which are unlikely to arise in the course of revaluing an existing swap portfolio but are common at the start of an off-market swap. We have made a number of simplifying assumptions: first, that the market movement creating an off-market situation takes place immediately after the swap position is created so that there are no accruals on the swap; and second, that the swaps themselves start on a coupon date so that all fixed coupons are the same.

Covered interest arbitrage

Returning to our original example of this type of swap, where we swapped currency B into currency A, we want to see what happens when both the market spot and forward rates change, from 1.000 and 1.0100 to 1.0300 and 1.0200 respectively. To liquidate the position we want to execute the reverse swap, selling currency B spot and buying it forward, and Figure 4.8 shows what happens when we do this, against a notional of 100 in currency B.

Figure 4.8a: Initial swap position

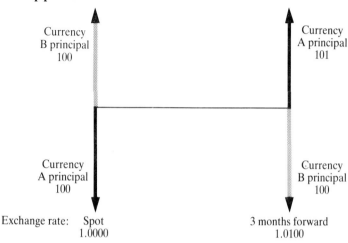

Figure 4.8b: Unwind of swap position at current market rate

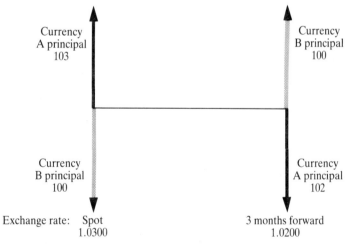

Figure 4.8c: Resultant position from unwind of swap

The net position after the unwind is that we are flat in currency B but in currency A we have a spot profit of A 3.00 and a forward loss of A 1.00. The value of the original swap is thus the present value of these two cash flows, which will be something over A 2.00, depending on the relevant interest rate in currency A. Since we are dealing with periods of less than one year there is no problem in choosing a reinvestment rate; it will simply be Libor. So valuation of an off-market structure is simply a matter of netting off the desired swap against the unwind at the current market rate and present valuing any resulting cash flows.

Long-term forward foreign exchange swap

The process for revaluing long-term foreign exchange swaps is virtually identical to that just described for covered interest arbitrage. Again, starting with our original example, Figure 4.9 shows the result of unwinding the position when rates have changed. What results is a highly irregular series of cash flows, whose present value is the revaluation profit or loss on the swap position. Because of greater maturity of the cash flows the choice of reinvestment method is more difficult.

Figure 4.9a: Initial long-term foreign exchange swap position

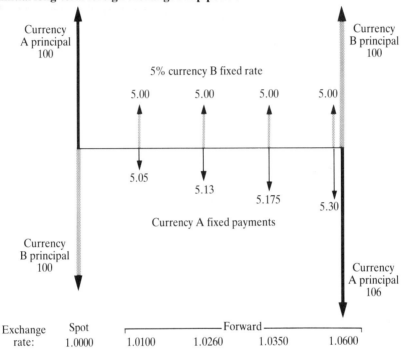

Figure 4.9b: Unwind of swap position at current market rates

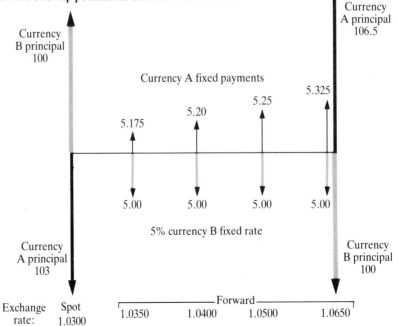

50

Figure 4.9c: Resultant position from unwind of swap

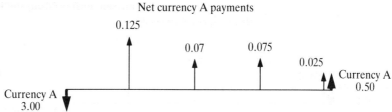

Net currency A payments

0.125
0.07
0.075
0.025
Currency A
0.50

Currency A
3.00

Floating to floating currency swap

A floating to floating currency swap will always have a nil revaluation at a coupon date (or refixing date) for both coupons, so long as in the original par-forward swap of principals there was an initial exchange. Figure 4.10 below shows the result of unwinding our original floating to floating example used earlier, now that the spot rate has changed from 1.0000 to 1.030:

Figure 4.10a: Initial floating to floating currency swap position

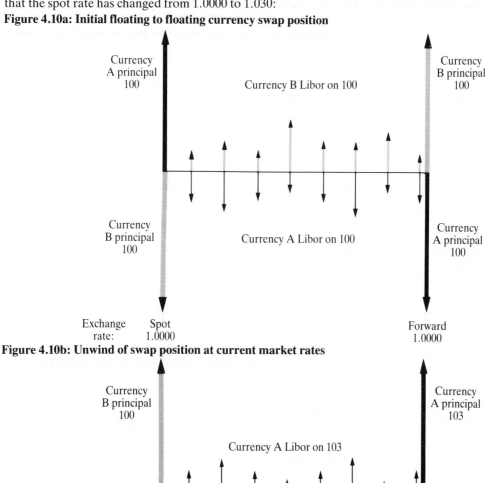

Currency
A principal
100

Currency B Libor on 100

Currency
B principal
100

Currency
B principal
100

Currency A Libor on 100

Currency
A principal
100

Exchange rate: Spot 1.0000

Forward 1.0000

Figure 4.10b: Unwind of swap position at current market rates

Currency
B principal
100

Currency
A principal
103

Currency A Libor on 103

Currency
A principal
103

Currency B Libor on 100

Currency
B principal
100

Exchange rate: Spot 1.0300

Forward 1.0300

Figure 4.10c: Resultant position from unwind of swap

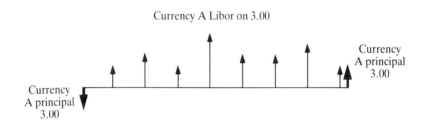

Currency A Libor on 3.00

Currency A principal 3.00

Currency A principal 3.00

As a result of the unwind we have a spot loss in currency A of 3.00 and a forward profit of 3.00, with intermediate cash inflows of Libor on 3.00. It is clear that the present value of these cash flows will be nil since to cover the spot loss we will have to borrow 3.00, and if it is borrowed on a floating rate basis then the interest payments will be matched by the net cash inflows from the swap unwind. Hence the revaluation of the original swap is nil, despite the change in exchange rates. Had there been no initial exchange of principals in the original swap and we used a par-forward swap with no initial exchange to unwind the position, then there would be no spot loss of 3.00, but the other cash flows would be unchanged, giving a revaluation profit of 3.00 from the position.

Fixed to floating currency swap

To show the types of off-market structure that can be created with fixed to floating currency swaps, we will consider three different revaluations arising from:

— a change in exchange rates only (equivalent to executing a swap with an off-market par-forward rate);

— a change in swap yields only (equivalent to executing a swap with an off-market fixed rate);

— a change in both exchange rates and swap yields (most commonly arising from an unwind of an existing currency swap position).

In each case we will use as our starting swap position the example of a fixed currency A into floating US dollars swap, with a par-forward rate of 1.5000 A to the dollar, a swap yield of 10 per cent and a US dollar swap principal of US$ 100.00, first used in Figure 4.5.

Off-market par-forward rate

If the market exchange rate is 1.3000 instead of 1.5000 and the market swap yield remains unchanged at 10 per cent then unwinding the swap will give residual cash flows in currency A since our object is to flatten all the US dollar cash flows, as in Figure 4.11. We will have left what looks very much like the arrow diagram for a long fixed rate bond position, costing 100 per cent with a coupon of 10 per cent since the change in the par-forward rate will affect all currency A cash flows equally.

Figure 4.11a: Initial fixed to floating currency swap position

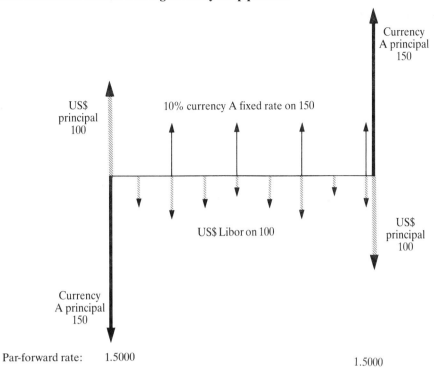

US$ principal 100

10% currency A fixed rate on 150

Currency A principal 150

US$ Libor on 100

US$ principal 100

Currency A principal 150

Par-forward rate: 1.5000

1.5000

Figure 4.11b: Unwind of swap position at current market exchange rates

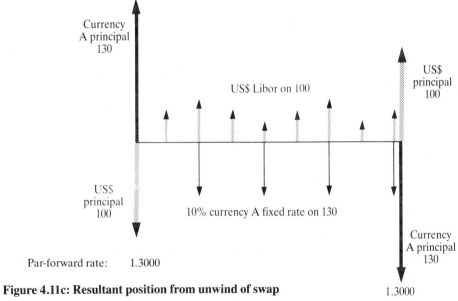

Currency A principal 130

US$ Libor on 100

US$ principal 100

US$ principal 100

10% currency A fixed rate on 130

Currency A principal 130

Par-forward rate: 1.3000

1.3000

Figure 4.11c: Resultant position from unwind of swap

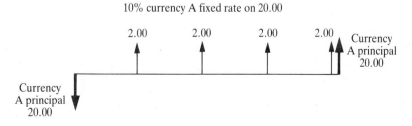

10% currency A fixed rate on 20.00

2.00   2.00   2.00   2.00

Currency A principal 20.00

Currency A principal 20.00

53

Using a discount rate of 10 per cent (since yields have not changed) the present value of this cash flow stream is nil. This result is very similar to the one we obtained in valuing the floating to floating currency swap, namely that the revaluation profit or loss is nil. This is hardly surprising, as we have deliberately removed interest rate risk in this example. What it shows, however, is that an off-market par-forward rate on its own does not affect the value of a swap.

Off-market swap yield

If the market swap yield in currency A is now 8 per cent instead of 10 per cent and the market exchange rate is left unchanged at 1.5000 then unwinding the swap has the result shown by the sequence in Figure 4.12.

Figure 4.12a: Initial fixed to floating currency swap positon

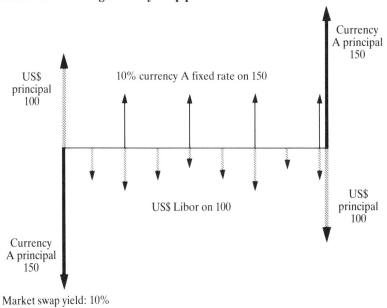

Market swap yield: 10%

Figure 4.12b: Unwind of swap position at current market yields

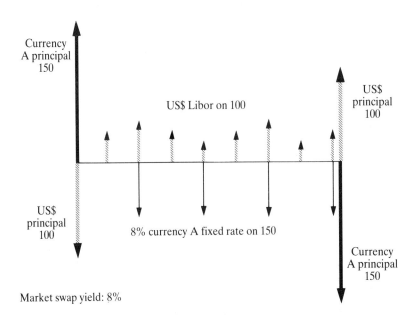

Market swap yield: 8%

Figure 4.12c: Resultant position from unwind of swap

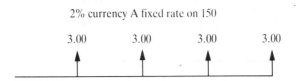

This result is similar to the case of unwinding an interest rate swap in US dollars; because the par-forward rate has not changed there might as well not have been a currency element to the swap at all. The net position is an annuity of 2 per cent pa on the currency A notional, and this has a present value of 6.62 per cent or A 9.94 when discounted at 8 per cent pa. Thus a change in yield of 2 per cent has increased the value of the swap by 6.62 per cent and, as shown earlier in Chapter 3, this is exactly the same revaluation profit as would arise on a long position in a 10 per cent currency A bond held for the same period (assuming that both bond and swap were being revalued on the same basis against the same interest rate environment).

As an off-market structure, this type of swap is most commonly used to hedge a foreign currency bond position into floating US dollars where the bond coupon differs from the market swap rate in that currency, with the object of exactly matching the swap fixed rate cash flows with the bond coupons. The up-front settlement is then the present value of the 2 per cent annuity, discounted at the appropriate reinvestment rate (discussed below), in exactly the same way as for an interest rate swap.

Off-market par-forward rate and off-market swap yield
If the market swap yield in currency A is now 8 per cent instead of 10 per cent and the market exchange rate has moved from 1.5000 to 1.3000 then the resulting revaluation is a compound of the two previous examples; because of the change in swap rate, the change in par-forward rate now begins to have a direct effect on the cash flows too, as shown by the sequence in Figure 4.13.

Figure 4.13a: Initial fixed to floating currency swap position

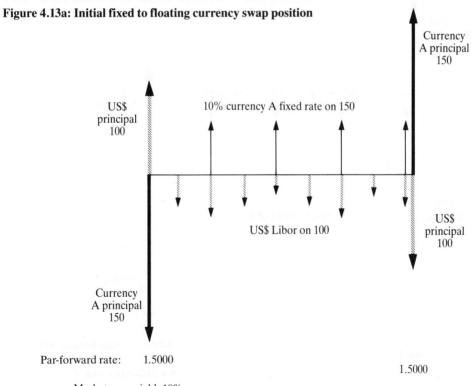

Figure 4.13b: Unwind of swap at current market yields and exchange rates

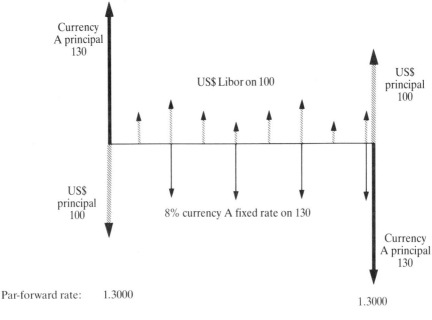

Par-forward rate: 1.3000

Market swap yield: 8%

Figure 4.13c: Resultant position from unwind of swap

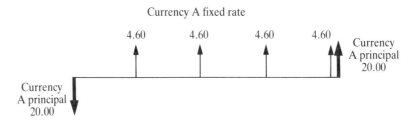

The final position resulting from the unwind now comprises the net position from our first unwind (when only the par-forward rate changed), the residuals from the par forward and some intermediate coupons, and a fixed rate annuity arising from the yield change. This cash flow effect is not simply additive (if it were then the coupons would be 2 and 3, ie a total of 5), because the change in par-forward rate influences the annuity stream which is calculated as 10 per cent of A 150 minus 8 per cent of A 130 equals A 4.6 pa. However, using a discount rate of 8 per cent pa gives a present value in absolute terms of A 9.936 which is identical to the revaluation profit when we kept the par-forward rate constant and changed only the yield. So although the change in par-forward rate has an effect on the absolute cash flows, it does *not* affect the the final revaluation profit or loss.

Now that we have shown that the revaluation on a currency swap is independent of the change in exchange rate it is clear that this makes it a very attractive instrument for hedging a fixed rate foreign currency bond position, so long as swap yields in that currency correlate closely to bond yields. Any revaluation on a bond position, reflecting a change in bond yields, will be offset by an equal and opposite revaluation on the swap used to hedge it into floating rate, whether US dollar or the local currency, since that too will be determined by the corresponding change in swap yields. In some currency markets, such as the ECU, swaps provide the only means of hedging bond positions (apart from using Libor, with the risks that that implies) as there are no government or equivalent securities available to the investor for this purpose.

Fixed to fixed

A fixed to fixed currency swap is simply made up of two fixed to floating currency swaps, and the revaluation is simply the sum of the constituent swap revaluations. This means that interest rate movements in *either* currency will generate a revaluation profit or loss, which may be determined using the procedures outlined above.

Currency swap reinvestment risk

The whole of of the previous section has been devoted to the problem of determining the exposures that result from taking a currency swap position, expressing the result in terms of the resulting cash flow streams. Where present values have been calculated, this has been done using the AIBD formula, discounting at the prevailing swap rate, so as to avoid complexity. In fact, this is exactly the same reinvestment problem as occurs with interest rate swaps as described in Chapter 3. However, that discussion focused mostly on the US dollar market, where there is a wide range of methods. In most other markets the choice is limited to either reinvestment at Libor, at the swap rate, or by using the implied zero coupon swap curve (except in sterling, Deutschemarks and Canadian dollars, where government securities may be used, although their usefulness as hedging instruments is limited owing either to a lack of liquidity or to central bank rules prohibiting short sales). Because the currency swap market is a more recent arrival on the swaps scene, many participants have moved on from using the swap rate, but most have not yet reached the implied zero coupon swap curve. Consequently, the vast majority still use a Libor reinvestment assumption, and manage the cash reinvestment or borrowing position as part of their overall cash pool. It seems reasonable to expect that as the currency swap markets become more competitive, more attention will be paid to this aspect of swap portfolio management.

SECTION 3

The Techniques

Section 3 addresses the mechanics of making synthetic securities and examines the effects of this activity on related markets.

Section 3 comprises 4 chapters:

Chapter 5 covers the three usual ways in which bonds can be combined with swaps to create synthetic securities, using the example of the synthetic US dollar floating rate note.

Chapter 6 expands on the simple example used in chapter 5 and provides a series of examples of different types of synthetic security explaining how they can be created by using different combinations of bonds and hedge techniques.

Chapter 7 is a case study on the market for Floating Rate Notes. In it we explain how investors became disillusioned with many of the innovations in the FRN market which were designed to benefit issuers, and we show how synthetic techniques can be used to recreate these "innovations" in a way which satisfies investors.

Chapter 8 examines the effects of the growth in the market in synthetic securities on related markets. In particular we discuss the fixed coupon Eurobond market, the markets for interest rate and currency swaps and the market for instruments which are direct substitutes for synthetic securities, such as publically issued FRNs and syndicated loans.

By the end of section 3 you will be able to design, structure, price and transact a wide range of types of synthetic securities, and will have sufficient conceptual understanding of the processes to enable you to create new variations.

CHAPTER 5
How to combine swaps and bonds

Introduction

This chapter is designed to explain how the instruments covered in Chapters 2, 3 and 4 can be combined or packaged to create synthetic instruments. We shall cover the process in which bonds and swaps are linked to generate wholly new financial instruments from the perspective of each of the parties concerned: the arranging bank, the swap provider, and the investor.

There are three ways in which a synthetic instrument can be presented for sale to an investor:

— as an ***asset swap*** in which the component parts are offered separately and usually simultaneously, in such a manner that the net cash flows and sensitivity to interest rates will replicate the performance of the desired resultant instrument;

— as a ***Synthetic Security,*** a new instrument structured so that the investor buys only those components of the underlying instruments which contribute to the desired performance or behaviour, without any unwanted elements which are usually retained by the arranging bank;

— as a ***special purpose vehicle issue of synthetic securities*** in which the arranger establishes a special purpose vehicle which holds asset swaps and which issues new securities backed by these asset swaps.

A brief history

Before we analyse each of these three techniques it is worth looking at the earliest attempts to create synthetic instruments.

The gilt swap

The first attempts to satisfy investor demand for investment instruments which did not exist in the marketplace, but which could be conceived of by combining existing, but at that time new, financial instruments, were all structured as asset swaps. The first asset swap is thought to have been executed in early 1980 for US investors who wanted a US dollar based fixed coupon instrument of top sovereign quality at a significant yield premium over then prevailing US Treasury yields. The transaction was called the gilt swap and was structured as follows:

The investor:

— liquidated a portion of his existing US Treasury note portfolio (fixed coupon US dollar denominated bonds, paying interest semiannually on an actual/365 day basis) in order to create sufficient liquidity for the new investment;

— sold US dollars spot for sterling and simultaneously entered into a long-term forward foreign exchange transaction in which he bought US dollars for sterling at a forward date. The counterparty would then attempt to reverse this forward foreign exchange position through the long-term foreign exchange market;

— used the sterling proceeds of the spot foreign exchange transaction to purchase a 5 year gilt (a fixed coupon sterling denominated bond, paying interest semiannually on an actual/365 basis, issued by the UK government);

— also entered into a series of forward foreign exchange contracts in which he agreed to pay to the counterparty a series of sterling cash flows, which exactly matched the sterling coupon receipts from his holding of the gilt. In return, he received a series of US dollar cash flows which, although not equal, as the forward foreign exchange rate varies over time, could be compared to the coupon payments of a US Treasury bond

Thus, the investor created a synthetic US dollar gilt which paid out a higher yield than was available on a straightforward investment in US Treasury notes.

This sequence of transactions can be illustrated diagramatically using the same cash flow convention introduced in Chapter 2, in which a down arrow represents a cash outflow, and an up arrow a cash inflow:

The five-year US Treasury note originally held by the investor would look much like this:

Figure 5.1: Five year US Treasury note

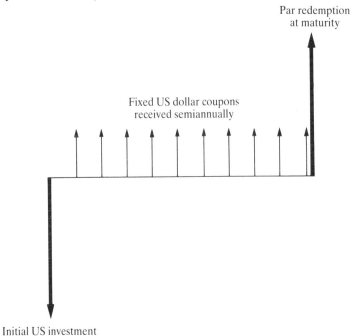

Liquidation of the US Treasury note position releases US dollars to pay into the spot exchange of the principal swap. The principal swap is shown in Figure 5.2.

Figure 5.2: Principal currency swap

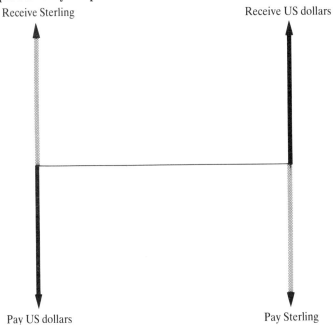

The spot sterling proceeds of the principal swap are then invested in a five-year gilt as shown in Figure 5.3.

Figure 5.3: Five year gilt

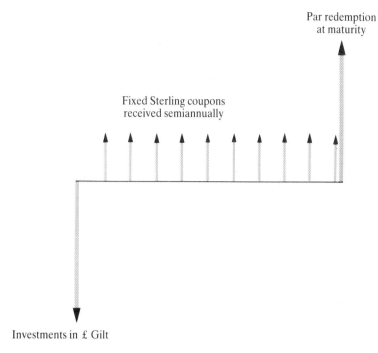

The swap of the sterling coupons in to US dollars (the coupon swap) is shown in Figure 5.4.

Figure 5.4: The coupon swap

The resultant investment has the following characteristics:

— proceeds of the US Treasury note sold exactly match the spot exchange of principal;

— sterling proceeds of the spot exchange in the principal swap exactly match the investment in gilts;

— sterling coupons from the gilt match the sterling payments into the coupon swap

Therefore, these three sets of cash flows can be removed from the analysis as they effectively cancel each other out. Combining these transactions results in the synthetic US dollar gilt shown in Figure 5.5, yielding more than the original US Treasury investment.

Figure 5.5: Synthetic US dollar gilt

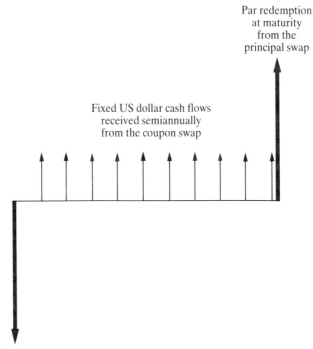

The synthetic US dollar gilt shown in Figure 5.5 is almost identical to the original five year US Treasury note shown in Figure 5.1 except for the higher yield that it provides the investor.

Yen bankers acceptances

A shorter tenor transaction — money market cross-currency discount swap — used the same principles, although with somewhat less complexity and had been practised for a number of years. In this transaction an investor has short-term currency to place for a period of typically not longer than six months in an instrument such as a bank issued negotiable certificate of deposit, bankers acceptance or commercial paper. If these instruments are not available in the currency in which the investor has surplus liquidity, or a higher yield can be obtained by investing via another currency, he can use a short-term currency swap on a covered interest arbitrage basis. This transaction is less complex than the gilt swap, as both the principal and interest components are hedged together by the foreign exchange swap; there is no separate payment of interest by a discount instrument.

The sequence of transactions in which a US dollar bankers acceptance of six months' maturity is hedged into a synthetic yen bankers acceptance is illustrated below:

— The investor liquidates a portion of his short-term yen holdings, or generates surplus liquidity as a result of one of these instruments maturing;

— sells yen spot for US dollars, so that the US dollar proceeds of the foreign exchange transaction will cover the purchase of a US dollar discount instrument such as a bankers acceptance, and simultaneously enters into a six month forward foreign exchange deal in which he sells US dollars for yen, so that the US dollar amount paid into the foreign exchange contract matches the redemption amount of the maturing US dollar instrument.

— purchases a high yielding six month US dollar bankers acceptance with the proceeds from the spot foreign exchange.

The original yen instrument which matured or was sold looked like this:

Figure 5.6: Original yen instrument

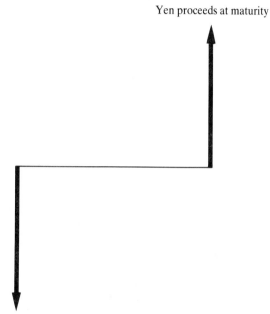

Yen proceeds at maturity

Initial Yen investment

The Spot and forward foreign exchange transactions in which yen is sold spot for US dollars and yen purchased forwards with US dollars:

Figure 5.7: Foreign exchange swap

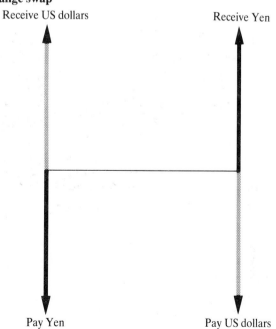

Receive US dollars   Receive Yen

Pay Yen   Pay US dollars

The US dollar discount instrument, in this case a bankers acceptance, bought by the investor:

Figure 5.8: US dollar bankers acceptance

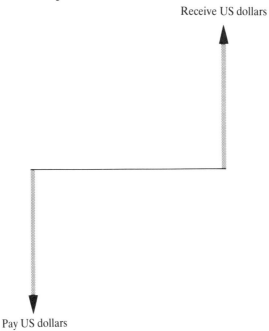

Receive US dollars

Pay US dollars

The yen paid into the foreign exchange swap generates US dollars which are invested in the high yield US dollar bankers acceptance. At maturity, the proceeds from the redemption of the bankers acceptance are used to meet the maturing foreign exchange contract which pays yen to the investor. The result is that the US dollar cash flows net out and the investor has only the desired resultant instrument, a high yielding short-term money market yen investment:

Figure 5.9: Synthetic yen bankers acceptance

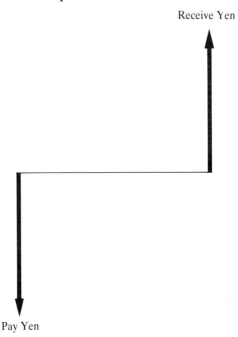

Receive Yen

Pay Yen

The investor has created a synthetic yen bankers acceptance which pays higher yields than available on alternative yen-denominated money market instruments, and has done this without entering into any foreign exchange risk. The two foreign exchange deals are not an exact swap, however, as there will be unequal amounts of US dollars on the spot and forward transactions. This will occur irrespective of whether the US dollar instrument pays interest by way of a discount in the current price compared to the redemption value, or pays explicit coupons; the investor must hedge his total return on the US dollars investment back into yen. This results in the foreign exchange swap counterparty ending up with a small spot position equivalent to the US dollar interest amount. This technique of covered interest arbitrage is well documented in the financial textbooks and will not be enlarged upon here.

These two transactions show that investors do not need to be either particularly sophisticated or intimately involved in current market trends to benefit from simple asset-based swap arbitrages, some of which have been practised successfully for many years.

Synthetic US dollar floating rate notes

Both of the examples described above are variations of asset swaps, in which, under the definition used at the beginning of this chapter, the component parts are purchased simultaneously but are accounted for separately. This section will examine the structure of the asset swap using as its model the most typical transaction, the US dollar floating rate note (FRN).

The US dollar FRN is created from a fixed coupon US dollar Eurobond combined with a US dollar fixed interest for floating interest swap. The basic elements which are used to create each of the asset swapped FRN, synthetic FRN and special purpose vehicle issue of synthetic securities are the same base Eurobond and fixed for floating interest rate swap. We shall cover the cash flows used in construction once only, and then analyse the three alternative construction techniques, focusing on the important differences between them.

The basic components are assembled as follows:

— A fixed coupon US dollar Eurobond is purchased in the market;

— A fixed for floating US dollar interest rate swap is entered into such that the fixed coupons from the bond exactly meet the fixed rate payments into the swap, and the bond and the swap mature simultaneously.

The purchased accrued interest on the bond is either funded until the next fixed coupon or is 'purchased' by the swap counterparty as one of the cashflows under the swap.

The fixed coupon Eurobond initially looks like this:

Figure 5.10: Fixed coupon Eurobond

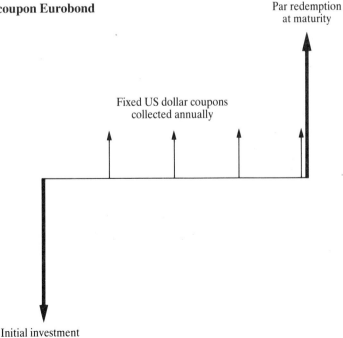

The fixed for floating US dollar interest rate swap looks like this:

Figure 5.11: US dollar interest rate swap

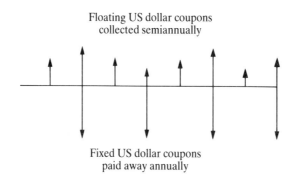

The coupons from the Eurobond can be 'stripped' from the bond as follows:

Figure 5.12: "Stripping" the fixed coupons

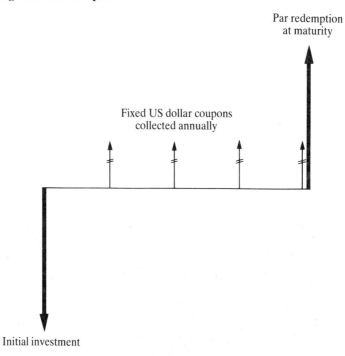

The fixed coupons can then be paid into the interest rate swap:

Figure 5.13: Pay fixed coupons into the swap

Resulting in the floating rate side of the interest rate swap being the only remaining set of cashflows, which can then be applied to the principal of the original Eurobond:

Figure 5.14: Resultant synthetic floating rate note

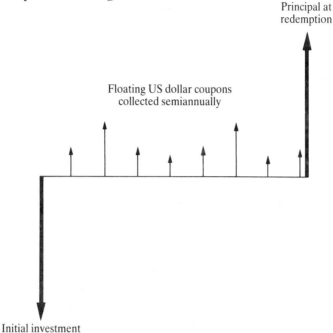

This basic construction of a Eurobond and US dollar interest rate swap is common to each of the asset swap, Synthetic Security and special purpose vehicle issue of synthetic securities.

The asset swap

This is sometimes referred to as the 'home-made' asset swap, because that is exactly what it is. The asset swap can be created by any institution with the relevant expertise, without any assistance from a third party in structuring the transaction. Figure 5.15 illustrates the payment streams over the life of an asset swapped US dollar FRN:

Figure 5.15: The asset swap

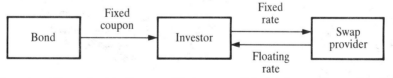

The investor is the central figure in this diagram. He is responsible for the purchase of a suitable bond and selection of a swap counterparty with whom to effect the interest rate swap.

In many cases an arranging bank assembles the component parts and offers them for sale to the investor as if they were a package. It is common in such situations for the arranger to be merely acting as an intermediator between the bond trader, swap provider and investor and such activity is typically run by the arbitrage department of the arranging bank. Due to the complex nature of swap accounting, cash flows and the credit sensitivity of swaps, arrangers rarely enter into the swap themselves but introduce the investor to a swap market maker who will provide the swap direct. This avoids the problem of having to assign the swap from the arranger to the investor. Figure 5.16 illustrates the role played by the arranging bank. When the sale to the investor is concluded the cash flows and contractual relationships are exactly as in the asset swap figure above, as the arranger drops out of the picture.

Figure 5.16a: Asset swap — the arranger's role, before sale to investor

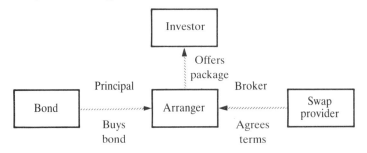

Figure 5.16b: Asset swap — after sale by arranger to investor

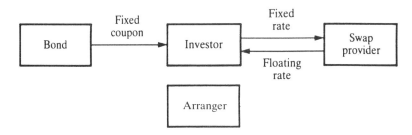

We will evaluate the asset swap using a framework which will be replicated when we go on to analyse synthetic securities and special purpose vehicle issues.

Cash flows

In the asset swap the investor has three distinct cash flows to manage. First, the fixed coupon from the bond has to be accrued and collected on the coupon payment date, whether annually, semiannually or more frequently. The investor is responsible for ensuring that accruals are processed on the correct basis, ie 360/360, actual/365, etc.

Second, the investor has to make payments to the swap counterparty. If the swap has been structured to exactly match the cash flows from the bonds, then the cash flows received from the bonds can be paid directly to the swap provider. Note that these funds will be received and paid away through different accounts and that the investor will be exposed to clean risk on the entire coupon payment for at least one day or until confirmation that the paying agent had released the coupon and it had been received in the investor's account.

Third, the final cash flow is the collection of floating rate interest, plus the agreed margin over Libor, from the swap provider on the Libor payment dates. US dollar Libor based accruals will be accounted for on an actual/360 basis.

Ownership and accounting

The investor owns the underlying Eurobond and must therefore account for it as an asset and reflect this in annual returns. He is also a principal to the swap and must account for this as a contingent obligation in his audited accounts. In order to achieve an entry in the accounts for a US dollar FRN, the investor has to revalue the bond and the swap so that together they equate to the FRN.

Revaluation is simple, as the prevailing secondary market price can be used. However, revaluing the interest rate swap is a more complex and less precise affair: even swaps market-makers differ in the way they account for swaps. There is no existing convention for the manner in which investors handle the accounting for distinct instruments which are purchased for aggregated performance, and this issue is one for the investor to discuss with his auditors. The typical solution is for one part of the transaction to be accounted for objectively (in the manner described above for bonds) and the other component(s) to have their revaluation adjusted so that the net sums to the intended resultant instrument.

Swap risk

The investor has both clean risk and counterparty risk on the swap provider. *Clean risk* is the risk that the swap provider will fail to make a payment when one is due and expected. This is essentially a cash management and funding issue and does not necessarily imply that a cancellation of the swap is imminent. Clean risk can be considered as the most the investor could lose as a result of payments not being made on any one day. *Counterparty risk* is the risk that the swap provider might default on the transaction at a time when the cost of replacing the swap in the market had risen substantially (ie the investor had made a gain on the swap and the swap provider default resulted in him failing to be able to recognise it). This risk is the 'cost to close' of the swap and for long-term swaps this risk can be very large.

The swap provider also has risk in respect of the interest rate swap on the investor for exactly the same amount and tenor, the only difference being that the cashflows are in the opposite direction. To this extent the swap risk can be thought of as *bilateral*, each party having equal and opposite risk on the other. This is illustrated in Figure 5.17.

Figure 5.17: Asset swap — risk relationships

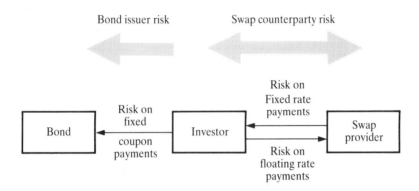

At any time during the life of the transaction only one side of the swap would actually face a cost of closing the swap, as the other party would have an equal and opposite gain. So although the swap risk is bilateral at the inception of the swap, as neither party knows the future course of interest rates, over time the cost to close will change in amount and may change direction.

Most swap market participants regard long-term swap risk as equivalent to an extension of credit, albeit in a diluted form, when compared to direct lending, and therefore entering into any swap will result in a usage of the investor's credit lines with the swap provider. Many investors similarly apply credit lines to swap providers and manage these risks actively, ensuring that they do not create too large a concentration of swap risk with too few swap market makers.

Credit risk

Credit risk is a complex issue which is fundamental to the appraisal of any type of security, be it a new issue or a home-made asset swap. To analyse credit risk fairly we will break out four separate components each of which contains an element of risk and evaluate them individually:

— principal of the bond;

— coupon stream paid by the bond;

— interest payments from the swap provider;

— cost of closing out the swap.

The investor has risk on the *principal* of the bond from the moment that he purchases it. That is, he stands to lose all, or part, of his investment if the bond issuer defaults. However, the investor also takes a clean payment risk on the amount invested when he purchases the bond. This risk is typically reduced by using one of the Eurobond clearing houses, CEDEL or Euroclear, and buying the bonds on a delivery against payment basis. The bond trader who sold the investor the bonds is obligated to deliver the bonds on the agreed value date and then receive payment. The clearing house ensures that the investor's funds are not paid away to the bond trader until good delivery of the securities can be effected. If the bond trader fails to make good delivery the investor's funds are not released, but the trade continues to stand on the original terms, and the bond trader will be obligated to deliver the bonds or risk being 'bought in' (a forced purchase of the bonds at whatever is the prevailing market price if the bonds are not delivered within 45 days). During the time that the trader fails to make good delivery the investor continues to have use of his funds and earns the coupon on the bond.

Similarly, the investor has *clean risk* on the *fixed coupon* stream which he expects to earn from holding the bond. This risk is the amount of each annual fixed coupon which the investor will be accruing during the year which he stands to lose if the issuer fails to make the payment. In addition, if the coupon payments are not made the investor will continue to be obliged to service the payments into the swap, otherwise the swap would terminate. So we can say unequivocally that the investor has *counterparty risk* on the fixed coupon payments which we could measure as the cost of replacing the coupons at prevailing market rates.

If the swap provider fails to honour his side of the swap agreement, and defaults on payment of the *floating rate* amounts, for whatever reason, the investor will incur losses. As the floating rate payments are made semiannually the amount that the investor can lose as a result of non-payment of a single amount tends to be smaller than for the swap provider (so long as two times Libor is less than the annual fixed coupon on the bond). So the investor's *clean risk* on the swap provider is for the amount of each semiannual Libor plus margin payment.

Finally, if the swap provider defaults on the payments under the swap it is likely that the swap agreement will have to be terminated and the investor may be faced with a substantial cost in *closing out the swap* at then prevailing market rates. However, it is worth noting that the incidence of swap cancellations as a result of default by one of the participants is extremely rare.

In summary, the investor bears risk on all aspects of the transaction.

Liquidity

The other issue which concerns the prospective investor in any type of security, be it a public issue, private placement or home made asset swap, is that of the liquidity of the instrument once it has been purchased. To some extent there is a trade-off between the yield a security offers and the ease with which it can be traded in the secondary market. To analyse liquidity we shall use two broad headings, *availability* and *cost* of liquidity, for each part of the asset swap, the Eurobond and the interest rate swap. The availability of counterparties who are willing and able to trade in the instrument is a prime determinant of the ease with which it can be divested; however, having numerous market makers is not sufficient to ensure that the cost of disposing of the instrument is not prohibitive.

Eurobond liquidity

Availability of liquidity

Eurobonds vary in the number of market makers they may have — from up to 20 for particularly liquid and actively traded issues to no market makers at all, in which case bonds tend to be traded on a 'bid only' or 'subject' basis.

Cost of liquidity

The cost, in terms of a market makers bid-offered spread, will vary from as little as 3/8 per cent for a liquid Eurobond to as much as 2 per cent for the most illiquid bonds, if a 'price' can be obtained at all. For the type of relatively illiquid bonds which are typically used as the source for asset swap transactions it is not unusual for the traders to quote prices on a bid-offered spread of between 3/4 per cent (three quarters of one per cent) to 1 per cent.

Interest rate swap liquidity

Availability of liquidity

There are a number of counterparties who claim to make markets in interest rate swap. Some of these market participants have trading books from which they are continually prepared to quote two-way prices for interest rate swaps of any maturity. These players are said to have 'swap warehouses'. However, the number of participants who run these warehouses is surprisingly small, especially for the non-standard non-US dollar swaps. However, for the purposes of the US dollar asset swap we have access to the broadest and deepest interest rate swap market in which at least 20 market makers truly exist. There is one caveat in terms of availability of interest rate swap market makers.

Both of the parties to an interest rate swap have counterparty risk on each other. To be able to execute an interest rate swap so as to reverse or cancel the previous swap, the investor must be able to obtain swap approval credit lines from the swap market maker, and in turn, be prepared to extend equivalent credit lines to the swap market maker. Finally, an investor should remember that if the swap is reversed with any market maker other than the one with whom the original swap was transacted he will have ongoing swap counterparty risk on both counterparties and they will similarly have risk on the investor and will consider this risk to be an allocation of credit lines until the swap matures.

Cost of liquidity

The bid-offered spread for US dollar interest rate swaps varies from 15 to 20 basis points in yield terms. That is 0.15 to 0.2 per cent per annum over the life of the swap. In present value terms, so as to be equivalent with the cost of liquidation used for the Eurobonds, this ranges from 0.8 per cent to 1½ per cent depending upon the tenor of the swap (longer tenors increase the present value amount, i.e. are more expensive to unwind) and the discount rate used in the present value calculation (it is usual to use either the yield on the bond or to discount the swap cash flows from the zero coupon curve as discussed in Chapter 2, irrespective of the rate base used lower discount rates which will increase the present value amount, again making the swap more expensive to unwind).

Asset swap liquidity — Eurobond and interest rate swap combined

Availability of liquidity

There is probably no more than one counterparty who would be prepared to provide a price for the combination of the bond and swap in its form as an asset swap; the arranger of the transaction if the asset swap was brought to the investor as a package by a third party. However, frequently such intermediaries are not swap market makers themselves and therefore are unable to provide a price for the package. The investor has at least the bond market makers and interest rate swap warehouse managers to approach for prices on each component of the asset swap as discussed above. The one area which may give some cause for concern is that any timing differences in divesting of the bond and the swap may result in unforseen gains or losses. Recently, with the advent of industry-wide, standard documentation, asset swap packages have become more liquid as the swap component can be easily assigned (subject to the credit quality of the new investor).

Cost of Liquidity

The combined cost of liquidating the bond and the swap can be expected to range from a minimum of 1.175 per cent (⅜ per cent + 0.8 per cent) to 3.5 per cent (2 per cent + 1.5 per cent). These figures explicitly ignore any gains or losses resulting from non-simultaneous divestment as discussed above.

Market developments

Before embarking on an in-depth analysis of the Synthetic Security it is worth considering other structures which have been developed in an attempt to solve the problems posed by the asset swap — too many cash flows, too much accounting and too little, too expensive, liquidity.

The first modification from the asset swap was for the arranger to enter into the swap itself as principal and then to assign the swap to the investor when the sale was effected. This development allowed the arranger to 'warehouse' the asset swap on his balance sheet and thereby benefit from creating asset swaps when market conditions were favourable, irrespective of the prevailing demand from investors. These packages were sold at a later date and the sale was effected by selling the investor the bonds and assigning the swap. This construction results in either the swap provider being prepared to formally cancel the original swap with the arranger and book an identical swap with the new investor, or the arranger retaining the original swap and writing an identical swap with the investor. In the first case the swap provider must be able to obtain credit approval against both counterparties — the arranger and then the investor — and be willing to re-book the swap in this way.

For most asset swaps the transaction size tends to be small when compared with typical swap market deal sizes and therefore swap providers typically took the view that obtaining two swap approvals and booking a small deal twice in order to allow a competitor to service an investor, who would be known to both parties, had little value. In the second case, in which the arranger intermediates the swap through to maturity, the arranger introduces his own credit risk into all the swap payments in addition to those risks discussed above. The trade-off from the arranger's standpoint is in retaining the investor's anonymity from the swap provider and in being able to substitute the arranger's credit standing for the investor's with the swap provider, thereby allowing the arranger to service investors either unknown to the swap provider or of insufficiently good credit quality to satisfy his credit approval process.

This second route met with some popularity in the initial stages of the market's development and arrangers developed a sales structure modelled on the loan sales technique of selling subparticipations, rather than swap assignments, to effect these trades. The move from assignments, in which the arranger retains a degree of risk and therefore cannot remove the asset from his balance sheet, to subparticipations, in which, under strict accounting rules, the arranger can deem the trade to be a sale and therefore remove the asset from the balance sheet is a mirror of the activity at that time in the asset trading or loan sales areas. However, this phase was a temporary step on the route to the market's maturity as, again in parallel to the loan sales market, a fully securitized instrument was in development.

In the case of loan sales, subparticipations gave way to transferable loan certificates (a partially tradeable instrument) which in turn were superseded by the mainstream of market activity by first Euronotes and then (fully tradeable) Euro commercial paper. In the asset swap market the first home-made asset swaps gave way first to asset swaps arranged by a third party and transferred by assignment, followed by asset swaps warehoused by an arranger and sold by subparticipation, which was finally superseded by the fully securitized form, the Synthetic Security.

The Synthetic Security

The Synthetic Security uses a different construction to the asset swap, but its aim is to create the same resultant instrument. The principal difference is the way in which this is done and the relative amount of effort expended by the investor and the manufacturer. The intention behind the creation of the Synthetic Security is to give the investor all the benefits of the asset swap in terms of high yield and tailor-made cash flows without the complexities of managing and accounting for separate instruments.

Figure 5.18 represents the payment streams between the parties over the life of the Synthetic Security

Figure 5.18: The Synthetic Security

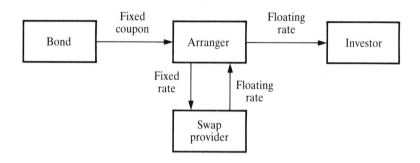

The investor is no longer the central figure: this role has been taken by the arranger who is now managing the purchase of the bonds, the bond fixed coupons and all the cash flows relating to the swap. The investor's only responsibility is to receive the floating rate payments from the swap counterparty as they fall due.

Cash flows

The arranger has to:

— accrue the fixed coupon from the bond on the correct basis;

— pay the swap provider the agreed fixed rate;

— collect the floating rate from the swap; and

— pay the investor the floating rate plus agreed margin.

The investor has to collect the floating rate Libor payments plus the agreed margin over Libor from the arranger on the Libor payment dates.

Ownership and accounting

The legal structure most commonly used in the creation of synthetics is for the arranger to sell the investor only those elements of the various components of bond and swap used in the creation of the synthetic which combine to provide the performance of the desired instrument. This means that for the synthetic US dollar FRN, the investor 'buys', and therefore takes ownership of, only the bond principal and the floating rate coupon paid by the arranger. The surplus cash flows are not sold by the arranger but are retained by him through to maturity. The most important of these is the fixed rate coupon being collected direct from the bond. As the investor buys only those elements which go towards the make-up off the resultant instrument, accounting should be only for the synthetic, and, unlike the asset swap, not for the component parts which were used in its construction.

Swap risk

The interest rate swap booked for a Synthetic Security is booked by the arranger against the bond issuer rather than against the investor. This mechanism yields two important benefits:
— The arranger does not utilise the investor's credit lines in approving the swap risk; and
— as the arranger has no swap risk on the investor he is indifferent as to the creditworthiness of the investor.

This second point has important implications for the secondary market liquidity of Synthetic Securities as we shall see in due course.

Unlike the asset swap in which the investor and arranger have bilateral risk on each other, in the Synthetic Security the swap risk on the bond is taken by the arranger and the swap risk on the arranger is taken by the investor, as follows.

Figure 5.19: The Synthetic Security — risk relationships

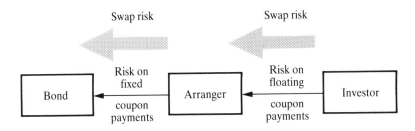

The investor is not a principal to the interest rate swap transaction which is, in effect, booked on his behalf by the arranger. However, he is the prime beneficiary of the swap and under the terms of the sale of the Synthetic Security the investor will be made responsible to the arranger for any costs which the arranger may incur on his behalf. So although the investor appears to be distanced from the swap counterparty risk on the payments of fixed coupons by the bond issuer the arranger will pass these costs on under the terms of the sale agreement.

The arranger books the interest rate swap against the bond issuer, but this does not mean that the investor is exonerated from any risk in respect of the arranger's receipt of fixed rate coupons. The arranger will view the booking of swap risk against the issuer as his *first way out*, that is the way in which he expects to get paid in the first instance if nothing goes wrong. However, the arranger will not be able to assume default risk on the bond and achieve an effective sale under most accounting conventions. By retaining residual risk on the bond, the transaction will not be considered to be a sale as the arranger will not have passed on all the risks and rewards of the transaction to the investor.

The arranger's *second way out* is to make non-payment of the fixed rate coupons an event of default under the sale agreement and to look to the investor to make up any shortfall. This may be further backed up by the arranger taking security on the bonds which it holds in custody on behalf of investors, and, as a *third way out*, being able to realise this security. So, if an issuer has failed to make the fixed coupon payment and the investor has refused to meet either the coupon payments or the costs of closing out the swap, the arranger may liquidate the investor's bonds in the market in order to cover his close-out costs. This structure may appear to be very onerous on the investor but it must be remembered that the investor still has no more risk in respect of the swap than under the asset swap.

Credit risk

As the investor purchases the principal of the bond he undoubtedly has risk on it should the issuer go into default, for whatever reason. The bonds which are used as the backing for Synthetic Securities are usually held in custody by arrangers on behalf of investors (remember that the arranger has title to the fixed coupon stream as this has not been sold to the investor); the investor does not have clean delivery risk on the bonds when they are purchased from the market.

Although the investor does not take title to the fixed coupons paid by the bond he will, however, be responsible for covering the arranger's costs in the event of non, or partial, payment by the issuer. This can happen in one of two ways:

— The investor makes up any shortfall should the bonds fail to pay in full out of his own pocket, and continues do to this through to the maturity of the synthetic. If the arranger allows the investor to do this he will be changing the Synthetic Security into an asset swap and will therefore be obliged to obtain a swap approval against the investor.

— Alternatively, the investor may decide to pay any close out costs resulting from the termination of the swap.

In addition, as was pointed out above, the arranger may have taken security against the investor's bonds to protect himself against non-payment by the investor.

These two methods are equivalent in monetary terms; the former is an annuity stream of the coupons, the latter is the same annuity stream discounted to a present value amount. However, it is usually at the discretion of the arranger to determine if he is prepared to offer the former alternative as it predicates an availability of swap lines.

If the arranger defaults in payment of the floating rate amounts, for whatever reason, the investor will incur losses. In addition, if the arranger defaults on any payment, or goes into bankruptcy proceedings, the investor should consider that the arranger has taken ownership of the fixed coupons from the bond. The investor will be in the position of general creditor of the arranger for those coupons which have gone unpaid.

Finally, if the Synthetic Security is terminated there may be a cost of closing out the interest rate swap in the market. Such costs are inevitably for the account of the investor.

To summarise, the investor bears risk on all aspects of the Synthetic Security package, despite the fact that he does not own all the component parts, and therefore the risk profile from the investor's point of view is broadly similar to that of the asset swap.

Availability of liquidity

As the Synthetic Security is a packaged financial instrument it would appear unlikely that a broad secondary market would exist. However, due to the subtleties of its construction it is possible for an investor to sell a Synthetic Security to another investor without any difficulty.

There is probably only one counterparty who could be considered to be a market maker in Synthetic Securities and this would be the investment bank which sold the investor the Synthetic in the first place. Due to the construction of the Synthetic the original arranger has no ongoing swap risk. Because of this, the arranger will be indifferent if an investor sells the package of bond plus swap to any other investor. Therefore, the number of counterparties who could purchase a Synthetic Security must include all those investors who have already bought Synthetics.

For an investor to sell a Synthetic Security he must first contact a likely buyer, offer the Synthetic package, subject to the new investor accepting the arranger's standard documentation, and agree a price. Upon confirming commitment by both parties to buy and sell respectively on the agreed terms, the original owner contacts the arranger and advises that he has sold the Synthetic to a new counterparty and advises the new owner of payment details. If the buyer is an existing client of the arranger nothing further occurs. If, however, the buyer is not a client of the arranger the arranger will send standard documentation to the new buyer.

Figure 5.20 illustrates the cash flow resulting from the secondary market sale.

Figure 5.20: Synthetic Security — secondary market sale

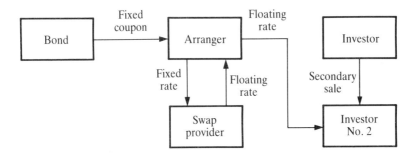

Note that the original construction of the Synthetic Security remains unchanged as a result of the sale by the original investor in the secondary market. The floating rate payments from the arranger are now redirected to the new investor when due. This simple way of effecting secondary market liquidity has important implications for the cost of liquidating a holding of a Synthetic Security.

Cost of Liquidity

As was pointed out in the previous section on the availability of secondary market liquidity, the bond and swap which have been linked together to form the Synthetic Security are not separated when sold by an investor, but are transacted as a package. This avoids the investor being exposed to both the bid-offered spread on each of the interest rate swap and on the underlying bond. Consequently, the Synthetic Security trades on a similar basis to the instrument which it behaves like, in the case of our example, a US dollar floating rate note. FRNs typically trade on a 3-5 basis point (three to five hundredths of one per cent) spread in yield terms which equates to a present value, or price, spread of between ⅛ per cent and 0.15 per cent depending upon the tenor of the Synthetic Security and the prevailing level of interest rates used to discount the per annum spread.

Special purpose vehicle issue

Here, the transaction is structured in a manner similar to the Synthetic Security discussed above, in so far as the investor does not enter into separate contracts to purchase each of the underlying bond and the US dollar interest rate swap. The principal differences are as follows:

— the arranger establishes a special purpose offshore vehicle (SPV), usually in Jersey or Cayman, whose sole function is to accommodate an issue;

— the SPV purchases many different bonds with matching swaps from the arranger on an asset swap basis;

— the SPV does a public issue of a bond, usually lead managed by the arranger, whose performance is determined by the composition of the bonds and swaps the SPV owns.

The SPV has assets of bonds and swaps which it has purchased on an asset swap basis and has liabilities to investors of bonds which are equivalent to the portfolio of asset swaps.

Figure 5.21 represents the payment streams between the parties over the life of the special purpose vehicle issue of synthetic securities:

Figure 5.21: SPV issue of synthetic securities

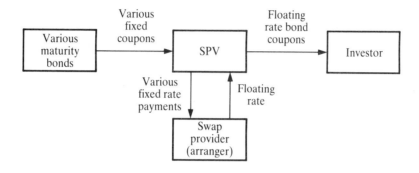

An alternative way to analyse the special purpose vehicle issue of synthetic securities is to look at the principal flows and the relationships between the parties, as follows:

— the SPV buys a portfolio of bonds with various maturities from the arranger;

— the SPV books interest rate swaps with the arranger so that all the fixed rate payments coincide with the expected inflow from the bond, and so all floating rate receipts occur on the same six monthly cycle;

— the arranger leads a public issue in the Euromarkets for the SPV; and finally

— the arranger places the bonds issued by the SPV with investors (see Figure 5.22).

Figure 5.22: SPV issue — responsibilities

This shows much more clearly the role of the arranger who is instrumental in setting up, administering, lead managing and selling the issue to investors. The special purpose vehicle can be seen here in its correct context as both a device for the arranger to effect sales of asset swaps to investors and make these look like Synthetic Securities with all the associated benefits of simple accounting and low cost liquidity.

Cash flows

The special purpose vehicle has to:
— accrue the fixed coupons from each of the bonds in its portfolio on the correct basis;
— pay the swap provider the agreed fixed rates when due;
— collect the floating rate payments from the swap; and
— pay the investor the floating rate plus agreed margin.

The arranger has to:
— establish and administer the SPV over its life ,which, barring defaults, usually coincides with the life of the longest maturity bond;
— sell the SPV a portfolio of fixed coupon bonds;
— book a series of matching swaps with the SPV in which the arranger receives fixed rate payments and pays floating rate;
— lead manage a bond issue for the SPV of bonds which are either backed or collateralised by the portfolio of bonds and swaps owned by the SPV; and
— place these bonds with investors.

The investor has to collect the floating rate Libor payments plus the agreed margin over Libor from the arranger on the Libor payment dates.

Ownership and accounting

The special purpose vehicle owns a portfolio of bonds and a series of matching swaps which it has bought from the arranger on an asset swap basis (ie as separate bonds and swaps). As the SPV is an offshore vehicle, the accounting regulations applicable are not necessarily consistent with those in the major financial centres, and as the vehicle is not going to be consolidated onto the legal books of a corporate entity this allows use of local conventions. Furthermore, as the SPV has liabilities, in the form of the bonds issued, which are designed to be exactly equal to the portfolio of asset swaps which it owns, as long as both sides of the balance sheet are accounted for on a consistent basis the SPV will have no net worth beyond the few hundred US dollars of original capital. Technically the SPV has two choices — to account for the bonds and swaps on the basis of realisable value (ie the prevailing market bid price for the bonds and the close out costs of the swaps) or to select some other value which is consistent with valuing the SPV on a going concern basis.

The investor owns a floating rate bond issued by the SPV which is backed by the portfolio of asset swaps owned by the SPV. Therefore, the investor may value his investment in these bonds on the basis of the prevailing market bid price without any concern about the complexities of swap accounting. This feature of the special purpose vehicle issue of synthetic securities is perhaps its most attractive as it allows the complex accounting and cash flow management issues to be concentrated in the SPV, leaving the investor owning a simple instrument (a floating rate bond) which has the performance and yield of a synthetic security.

Swap risk

The investor has no direct risk on the swaps as he is not a principal to any of the swaps transacted by the SPV. It is as if the SPV is standing in for the investor and intermediating the swap booking and accounting for him. However, as the bonds owned by the investor are issued by a vehicle with negligible net worth, it is wise for the investor to be aware that any costs borne by the SPV in connection with the swaps will be passed on to him in the market price of his bonds. Hence, an analysis of the swaps risk taken by the SPV is necessary.

The SPV has risk on the arranger with whom all the swaps are most usually booked. If the swaps are booked with other swaps market makers the arranger would generally be obliged to provide some form of credit backstop as a result of the SPV's low capitalisation.

The arranger has swap risk on the SPV to the extent that the SPV may fail to make fixed rate payments when due. This is only likely to happen if either:

— bond held by the SPV fails to make a fixed coupon payment when due; or

— the legal structure under which the SPV has been incorporated is changed, for example if withholding tax was imposed

The arranger offsets both of these risks by having the SPV established as a separate entity in its own right, so that any costs borne by the SPV as a result of default by bond issuers or changes in the legal environment will be chargeable against the SPV's assets. As the SPV has no capital with which to absorb these costs this will have the immediate effect of reducing the value of the floating rate bonds issued by the SPV.

Figure 5.23 illustrates that the swap risk between the arranger and the SPV is bilateral, wheras the investor has risk on the SPV, and through the SPV, as it has no capital cushion, on the arranger:

Figure 5.23: SPV issue — risk relationships

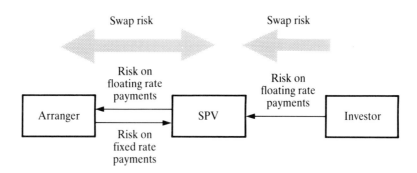

Credit risk

Due the nature of special purpose vehicle issues of the synthetic securities, in which the investor owns floating rate bonds backed by fixed rate bonds, the credit risk we are most concerned with is not the credit worthiness of the floating rate bonds issued by the SPV but the credit quality of the underlying portfolio. This is especially so as the SPV has insufficient capital to absorb any losses incurred within the portfolio.

The principal of the bonds Although the investor does not have a direct claim on the underlying bonds held by the SPV he undoubtedly has credit risk on them as a default by one of the bonds will immediately reduce the value of his investment in the floating rate bonds issued by the SPV. The investor does have one advantage by investing in asset swaps via the SPV; the investor has a share in a large, diverse bond portfolio which should serve to disperse credit risk on individual components of the portfolio. Theoretically this should allow a lower average credit quality and therefore higher yield. In practice, while the average credit quality may be lower, the yield is not higher than asset swaps of comparable quality.

The coupon stream paid by the bond Again, the investor has risk on the fixed coupon payments owed by the portfolio of bonds.

The interest payments from the swap provider If the swap provider fails to honour his obligations to make payments of the floating rate amounts when due the investor will again suffer losses through the market value of the floating rate bonds.

The cost of closing out the swap Finally, if the swaps are closed out by the SPV the investor will bear all the costs. However, due to the securitized structure of the special purpose vehicle issue of synthetic securities the investor does not have any say in how this is done, nor will he be able to make the decision to make the fixed rate payments himself.

In summary, the investor, although he is not a principal to any part of the portfolio of asset swaps, is exposed to risk on all aspects of the transaction.

Availability of liquidity

The investor need only concern himself about the number of counterparties willing to purchase the floating rate bonds issued by the SPV, and so long as a reasonable number of these exist need not be concerned about the SPV's assets being liquidated on a forced sale basis. The recent issues of bonds backed by bonds have met with good demand in the primary market and are said to be well placed. Secondary market making is typically only by the arranger as it is only he who has the in-depth knowledge of the actual performance of each of the bonds in the portfolio and of the structure of the swaps transactions booked. Co-managers in the original issue have usually declined from making markets in these securitized hybrid instruments.

Cost of liquidity

On the basis that sufficient demand will exist for the floating rate bonds issued by the SPV through to the final maturity of the longest tenor bond in the portfolio, the investor's cost of liquidation is the bid-offered spread used by the market makers. This is typically between ¾ per cent and 1 per cent which is roughly equivalent to the spread used on the high yield securities which are held in portfolio by the SPV. This is clearly less onerous than the asset swap as the investor is not exposed to the cost of unwinding the swaps linked to the bonds. If, however, demand for these floating rate bonds in the secondary market is weak the bonds could fall to the level at which they could be profitably be unswapped and sold in the market as straight bonds.

Summary

The following table (5.24) summarises the most significant features of the three various types of synthetic security.

Figure 5.24: Comparison of synthetic securities

	Asset swap	Synthetic	SPV
Ownership	Components = Bond and swap	Resultant = New hybrid	Securitized resultant
Accounting	Bond and swap Separate for each component Complex	Synthetic Resultant Simple	New bond Resultant Simple
Swap risk	Bilateral investor on provider provider on investor	Unilateral investor on provider provider in issuer	Unilateral investor on SPV and arranger
Credit risk	All by investor	All by investor	All by investor
Liquidity	Market makers Bond = 1–20 Swap = 1–5	Market makers Synthetic = 1	Market makers Bond = 1
Availability	Counterparties = 20+	Counterparties = 100+	Counterparties = 50+
Cost	$\Sigma = 0.8\% - 2\frac{1}{2}\%$	$1/8\% - 0.15\%$	$3/4\% - 1\%$

CHAPTER 6
Types of synthetic security

Introduction

So far, we have looked at three different types of synthetic security — the gilt swap and yen bankers acceptances in Chapters 1 and 5 and the synthetic US dollar FRN in Chapter 5. Here we review a broader range of synthetic transaction structures, showing how different types of source bond can be restructured using some of the available hedge techniques and indicating the pricing features of both source bonds and hedges which prospective creators of synthetics should look for. Below is a check list of the structures covered in this chapter.

Currency linked synthetics

— Zero coupon bond created from a zero coupon bond in another currency or from a coupon bearing bond in the same currency;

— Dual currency fixed rate bond created from a fixed rate bond in either of the underlying currencies;

— Fixed rate bond with a currency option at redemption created from a fixed rate bond in the currency of the coupons.

Interest rate linked synthetics

— Capped floating rate note created from either a public FRN or a synthetic FRN;

— Minimax FRN created from either a public FRN or a synthetic FRN;

— Step-up/step-down FRN created from either a public FRN or a synthetic FRN;

— Drop-lock FRN created from either a public or a synthetic FRN.

Currency and interest rate linked synthetics

— Floating rate note created from a fixed rate bond in another currency;

— Capped floating rate note with optional currency redemption created from a fixed rate bond in another currency.

Currency linked synthetics

Zero coupon bonds

A zero coupon bond is one of the least complex financial instruments. It has no coupons, and therefore no accrued interest to purchase when trading in the secondary market. Its price is determined only by the present value of its one future cash flow, and is therefore simple to calculate. However, zero coupon bonds are not issued in many currencies, and are subject to confused tax treatment. These two factors create investor demand which cannot be satisfied from existing markets.

There are two principal ways of creating a zero coupon bond in a currency in which zeros have not been issued:

— 'Strip' the coupons from an existing coupon bearing bond in the same source currency as the required zero coupon bond and offer the cash-flows from the source bond as individual zero coupon bonds.

— Swap a zero coupon bond from another currency using a long-term foreign exchange contract.

We shall consider each method in turn.

Coupon stripping

The major disadvantage of coupon stripping for the prospective arranger of a synthetic zero coupon bond is the number of separate bonds generated. Each cash-flow from the source bond becomes a separate zero coupon bond in its own right, so, for example, a ten-year semi-annual bond will create twenty *coupon strips* (zero coupon bonds generated from the coupons only) and one, larger *principal strip* (the zero coupon bond generated by the redemption of the source bond at maturity)[1]. An example of the results of stripping a four year bond is illustrated in Figure 6.1.

Figure 6.1a: Four year fixed coupon bond

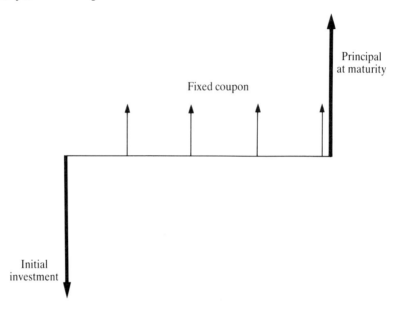

Figure 6.1b: One year coupon strip

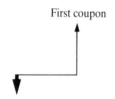

Figure 6.1c: Two year coupon strip

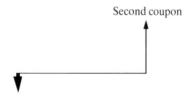

Figure 6.1d: Three year coupon strip

---

[1] However, since the last coupon normally coincides with the principal redemption, they may be combined into one strip, giving a total of twenty strips overall for the bond.

Figure 6.1e: Four year coupon strip

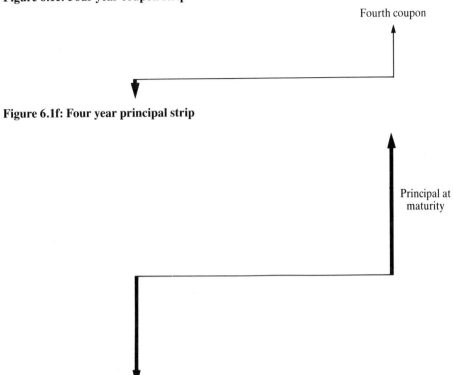

Fourth coupon

Figure 6.1f: Four year principal strip

Principal at
maturity

An alternative way to a strip a bond is to consider the coupons as a fixed rate annuity and the principal as the one-zero coupon bond. The relative simplicity of this approach is clearly seen by comparing the fixed rate annuity and principal strip in Figure 6.2 with the previous set of figures representing five separate zero coupon bonds:

Figure 6.2a: Four year fixed rate coupon bond

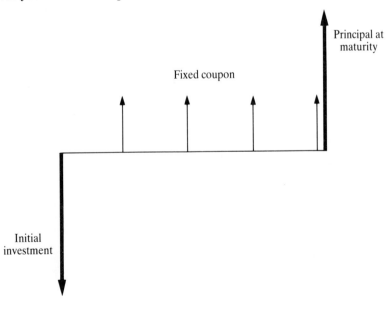

Principal at
maturity

Fixed coupon

Initial
investment

Figure 6.2b: Four year fixed rate annuity

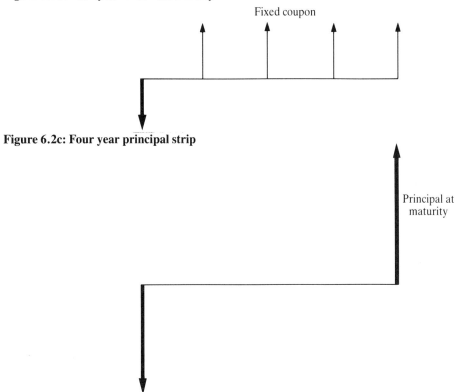

Fixed coupon

Figure 6.2c: Four year principal strip

Principal at maturity

In either case, an arranger intending to create one zero coupon bond with a specific maturity will find himself with a large residual if he uses the technique of stripping. This problem is further compounded for all coupon stripping exercises by valuing each individual cash flow off the implied zero coupon yield curve (see Chapter 3). The implied zero coupon yield curve is higher than the par yield curve for rising par yield curves and lower for falling par yield curves. (see Figure 6.3).

The zero coupon yield curve values *each* cash flow based upon *its* maturity. By contrast, the usual coupon (or par) yield curve values *all* the cash flows associated with a particular bond based upon the maturity of the *last* cash flow. This valuation technique provides the maturity or redemption yield calculations with which most investors are familiar. For a coupon stripping exercise to be succesful, the arranger must sell all the cash flows purchased at the maturity yield of the source bond at a higher weighted average yield (the weightings cover both amount and tenor).

For a rising but relatively flat par yield curves this is clearly a problem as the zero coupon yield curve will be above the par yield curve most of the time. For steeply rising par yield curves the weighted average yield on the zero coupon bonds sold is in theory not a problem. Also a steeply rising yield curve indicates that investors expect higher interest rates in future, they will therefore be unwilling to take additional interest rate risk by investing in long-maturity zero coupon bonds, which are highly sensitive to movements in interest rates without a substantial yield improvement over the implied zero coupon curve.

Cross currency zero coupon bond

The process of taking an existing zero coupon bond (either a public issue or the result of previous coupon stripping activity) in one currency and swapping it into a zero coupon bond in another currency is one of

Implied Zero coupon yield curves compared with source par yield curves

the most simple of the techniques used to create synthetic securities. It is identical to the money market discount swap using covered interest arbitrage discussed in Chaper 1 (yen bankers acceptances) and in Chapters 4 and 5 (covered interest arbitrage). The source bond is purchased by the arranger in US dollars and can be illustrated as follows:

Figure 6.4a: US dollar Zero coupon bond

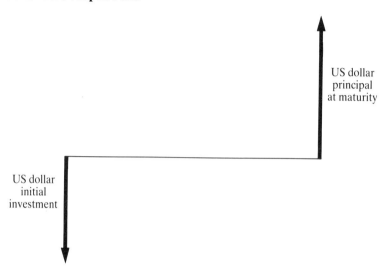

The hedge is no more than a pair of spot and forward foreign exchange contracts buying US dollars spot against the target currency, in this example Deutschemarks, and selling the US dollars and buying Deutschemarks forward for settlement on the same day as the source US dollar zero coupon bond matures. This foreign exchange transaction is commonly called a *foreign exchange* swap and is calculated by adding or subtracting an appropriate number of forward *points*, which represent the interest rate differential between the currencies at that future date, to the spot foreign exchange rate. The foreign exchange swap can be shown as follows:

Figure 6.4b: Foreign exchange swap

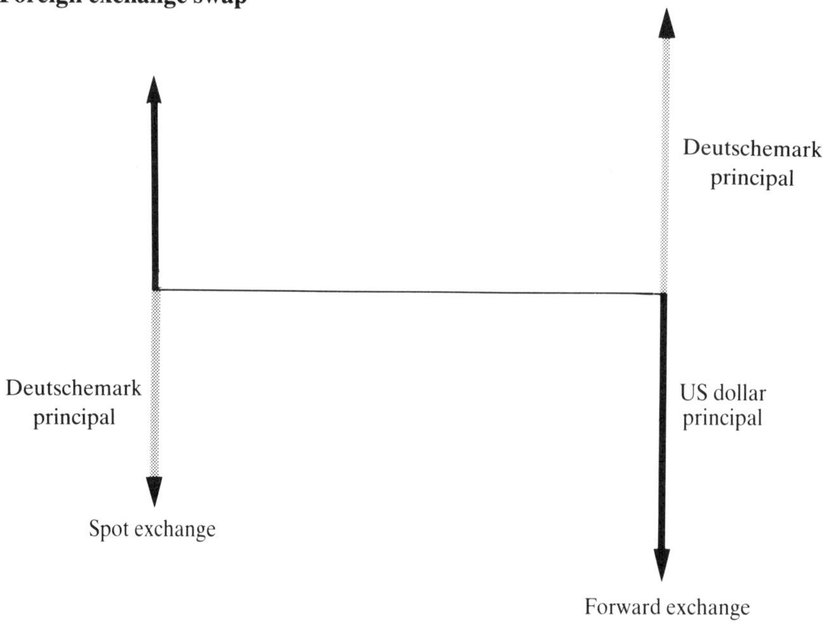

By combining the source US dollar zero coupon bonds with the foreign exchange swap all the US dollar cash flows net out, leaving the intended Deutschemark zero coupon bond behind. This can be shown as follows:

Figure 6.4c: Resultant Deutschemark zero coupon synthetic

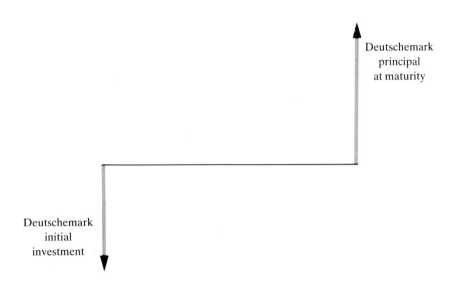

Credit risk; If the transaction is treated as an asset swap the investor will have risk on the issuer and on the mark to market value of the foreign exchange swap if the issuer fails to pay at maturity. Similarly, if the transaction is treated as a synthetic security the arranger will have direct exposure on the maturity proceeds of the source zero coupon bond, and on the mark to market of the foreign exchange swap if the issuer fails, as all these transactions will cross his books. However, as the investor is the beneficiary of the transaction, the arranger will usually pass on these risks to the investor under an appropriate legal agreement. Without these transfer of risk agreements the arranger would not be allowed, under most accounting conventions, to consider the transaction as an effective sale. Therefore he would not be allowed to take the source bond off his books with a consequent grossing up of the arranger's balance sheet.

Pricing; Arrangers should look for investor demand for currency zero coupon bonds at yields below the source zero coupon bond net of the adjustment for the interest differential between the currencies, as reflected in the forward points. There is little in the way of explicit arbitrage in this transaction as it is so simple; the value added comes from being able to create exactly the instruments that investors need.

Transacting the foreign exchange swap; Although the foreign exchange is usually called a swap, the arranger should remember that the amounts are not equal in either of the currencies as they are increased by the effect of aggregating interest over the life of the bond. The foreign exchange spot trader should be advised that he will have a residual spot position after the swap has been transacted with the forward foreign exchange dealer.

Dual currency bonds

Dual currency bonds are bonds with coupons (usually fixed), paid in one currency and principal at purchase and redemption paid in another currency. This dual currency features makes trading in the secondary market slightly more complex as, on any date other than a coupon payment date, the purchaser will have to pay not only the principal at the prevailing market price, but also accrued interest in the coupon currency. These bonds have on occasion been fashionable in the Eurobond market but have rarely been issued at times most suited to investors. The attraction in issuing these complicated bonds is for issuers to benefit from the difference between the forward discount *expected* by investors and the forward discount *quoted* by the long-term foreign exchange market of the principal currency against the coupon currency.

Issuers typically hedge away their currency risk via a long-dated foreign exchange contract so as to leave themselves with a single currency fixed coupon bond, which may, or may not, be further swapped into another currency or interest rate base. Investors find dual currency bonds attractive when they expect the principal currency to appreciate relative to the coupon currency by more than the implied forward foreign exchange rate. It might seem that issuers and investors have similar objectives from dual currency bonds as they both seek to earn the difference between the forward foreign exchange rate (implied by the interest rate differential between the currencies) and the expected forward foreign exchange rate. The fact is that this 'arbitrage' (between implied and expected forward foreign exchange rates) is taken largely by the issuer in a new issue, whereas it is taken largely by the investor in the creation of a synthetic dual currency bond.

The base bond is assumed to be a fixed rate Japanese yen denominated bond with four years to maturity, which pays annual yen coupons. It can be represented as follows:

Figure 6.5a: Source fixed rate yen bond

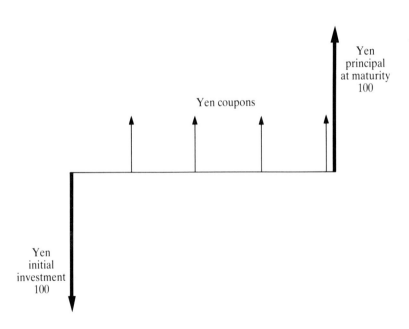

Investors believe that although the yen will continue to appreciate in relation to the US dollar, it is most unlikely that it will achieve a rate below 120 by the maturity of the bond in four years' time. The forward foreign exchange rate quoted in the market is 100 as yen interest rates are 4 per cent and US dollar interest rates are higher at 8 per cent. The arranger, who may be an investor for his own account, sells the yen bond principal for US dollars at a rate of 100 for forward settlement on the maturity date of the bond. The forward foreign exchange contract can be shown as follows:

Figure 6.5b: Foreign exchange swap

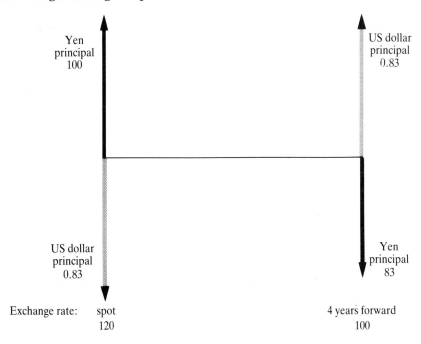

Yen
principal
100

US dollar
principal
0.83

US dollar
principal
0.83

Yen
principal
83

Exchange rate: spot   4 years forward
                   120   100

As the investor does not expect the US dollar to fall below 100 yen, a dual currency synthetic can be created with yen coupons collected direct from the source yen bond and with a US dollar redemption at 120 yen/US dollar. The cash flows of the bond and forward foreign exchange contract combined can be shown as follows:

Figure 6.5c: Synthetic dual currency bond without augmented yen coupons

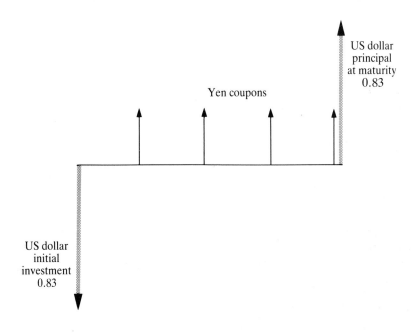

US dollar
principal
at maturity
0.83

Yen coupons

US dollar
initial
investment
0.83

This leaves the arranger with a surplus cashflow of 17 yen on the maturity date of the bond which is equivalent to the difference between the expected and implied forward foreign exchange rates. This surplus yen is used by the arranger to purchase an annuity stream (or endowment), in which the arranger will pay out equal amounts in yen on the coupon dates of the bond in return for collecting the surplus yen at maturity. The arranger takes an interest rate risk in executing this part of the transaction as he will have to fund the annuity payments through to collection of the lump sum at maturity (this risk can be hedged by an accumulating yen interest rate swap).

The reverse annuity can be shown as follows:

Figure 6.5d: Surplus yen at maturity

Figure 6.5e: Yen reverse annuity

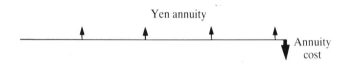

By combining the cash flows represented in the last two figures the two maturity amounts net out (as they are equal and opposite) and the arranger effectively uses the annuity to increase the yen coupons on the original source bond. This increase is created from the different view of the investor and the forward foreign exchange mark on the likely foreign exchange rate at the maturity of the bond. The resultant synthetic dual currency bond has higher yen coupons than the source bond and redeems in US dollars at 0.83. The arranger can now offer the principal of the bond in either yen or, after transacting a spot foreign exchange contract selling US dollars for yen, in US dollars. Accrued interest will still be payable by the investor in yen even if the principal is settled in US dollars.

Figure 6.5f: Resultant synthetic dual currency yen/US dollar bond

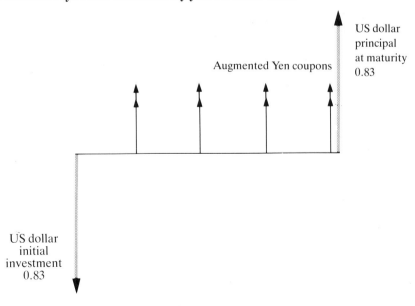

Credit risk The arranger has direct credit risk on the bond issuer for the future value amount of the annuity. This risk will have to be passed on to the investor who is the principal beneficiary of the transaction via a suitably worded legal agreement. The arranger also has counterparty risk in respect of the long term foreign exchange contract. This risk is on the investor if the transaction is arranged as an asset swap, or is on the bond issuer, secured by the bonds themselves, if the transaction is arranged as either a synthetic security or an SPV issue.

Advantages The alert reader will point out that all the investor has achieved is the inclusion in his portfolio of a long dated forward foreign exchange contract disguised in the form of a dual currency bond. This is correct. However, many investors are not able to reflect their foreign exchange views in their portfolios using forward outright foreign exchange contracts for a number of reasons. These might be internal limits which preclude portfolio managers from trading foreign exchange, although they may be able to trade in bonds of various currencies, including dual currency bonds. Similarly, the investor may only be allowed to buy listed instruments thereby excluding over-the-counter style foreign exchange contracts. Also, some investors would consider a 'naked' forward foreign exchange contract as unacceptably risky, in contrast to a dual currency bond which offers higher than market coupons. The principal advantage to the investor is one of timing. He is able to select exactly when to enter into the dual currency bond as he is no longer reliant on an issuer to issue in the currency and tenor he finds most attractive.

The principles of combining long-term forward foreign exchange contracts with bonds can be used to reverse an existing dual currency bond (either publicly issued or synthetic) so as to create a bullet, fixed rate, single currency bond. This technique is used to generate the market bid for most public and all synthetic dual currency bonds. The dual currency bond can be sourced from a bond in either the high or low interest rate currency. The low interest rate currency is most common due to the benefit of the forward discount, but if an investor expects appreciation over and above that implied by the forward foreign exchange market a synthetic could be created from a source bond denominated in the high interest rate currency. Also, a high interest rate source bond could be used for a conventional discount dual currency structure, but this is more complex to hedge as a series of forward foreign exchange deals would have to be transacted to create each coupon. As forward foreign exchange rates are seldom linear, this involves coupon smoothing and the attendant reinvestment risks (see Chapter 4).

Currency option linked bonds

Essentially, there are two types of currency option linked bond: those in which the investor has sold the issuer a currency option, and those in which the issuer has sold the investor a currency option. As investors have historically underpriced long-term currency options, structures in which investors have sold options have been most prevalent in the primary market. Investor knowledge of currency option pricing has improved markedly recently as a result of greater availability of long-term currency options, especially in the form of currency warrants, in the bond market. Consequently, investors have become net buyers of options rather than net sellers of options, and several bonds were issued in early 1987 with both embedded and distinct (in the form of warrants) currency options. With the increased maturity of the over-the-counter currency options markets, option expiries can be obtained out to five years. These longer maturities allow options to be linked to similar maturity bonds, in situations where the investor is either a buyer or a seller of options.

The example in Figure 6.6 shows an investor who requires higher coupons on a yen asset selling a US dollar call yen put, in order to generate premium income which the arranger reinvests and applies to the coupons in order to increase them.

The source bond is assumed to be a yen fixed coupon bond maturing in four years, which can be represented as follows:

Figure 6.6a: Source fixed rate yen bond

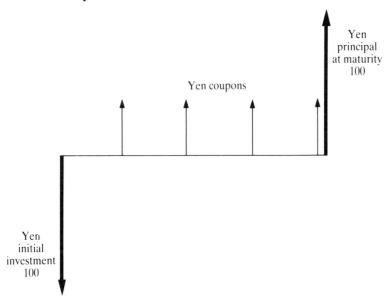

The arranger sells a currency option in which the holder has the right to buy US dollars and sell yen at a set exchange rate. This is shown in Figure 6.6b where the initial up arrow (positive cash flow) is the premium income in yen received for the sale of the option, and the dotted lines represent the conditional exchange at maturity:

Figure 6.6b: Yen/US dollar currency option

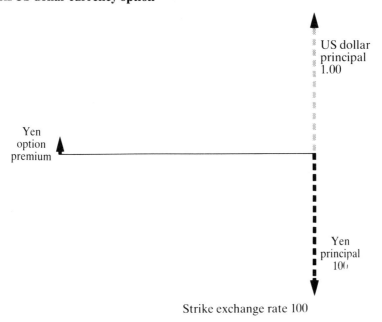

The arranger uses the yen premium income to purchase a yen annuity to increase the coupons on the source bond as follows:

Figure 6.6c: Yen annuity

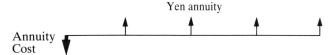

The final result is that the premium received for the currency option is used to pay for the yen annuity. The resulting high coupon yen bond will mature in either yen if the option holder does not exercise his option, or US dollars, if the option holder decides to exercise at a yen/US dollar rate which will be below the prevailing spot foreign exchange rate. The bond can be shown as follows:

Figure 6.6d: Resultant synthetic currency option linked bond

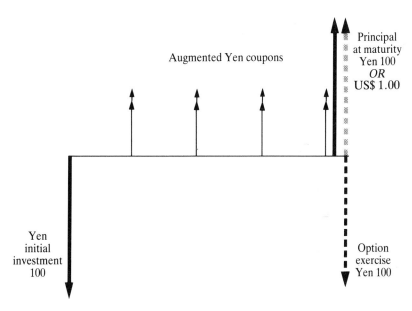

Exactly the same transaction can be constructed in reverse, with an investor accepting lower coupons in return for the right to receive the more valuable currency at maturity.

Credit risk The option buyer has direct exposure on the option writer through to the expiry of the option. This may result in few investors being able to write these long-dated currency options in order to enhance the yield on their portfolios. However, by transacting as a synthetic security in which the bond is held in custody by the arranger, and is used as collateral for this risk, investors can obtain access to the currency options market.

Interest rate linked synthetics

The fixed rate bond swapped in to a synthetic FRN by linking it to an interest rate swap in the same currency was covered in detail in Chapter 5 and will not be discussed again here.

Capped floating rate note

Restructuring an existing FRN in order to put a limit on its coupon payments is a simple transaction which can be used by investors to enhance the margin they receive over Libor (or whichever funding base is used). All the arranger does is to sell an interest rate cap contract and reinvest the premium income received in a fixed rate annuity stream which coincides with the coupons on the source FRN. As was the case with dual currency and currency option linked bonds discussed above, capped floating rate notes were first launched into the Euromarkets because investors undervalued the interest rate cap contract they had implicitly sold when buying the capped FRN. The issuer and lead manager shared the benefit of selling this cheap cap at a significantly higher price which more correctly reflected the cap's value. Investors are now more sophisticated in pricing bonds of all types which contain embedded options and are therefore better able to enter into these types of transaction in a way which ensures that they obtain fair value for the interest rate option sold.

In order to create a capped FRN the arranger purchases an FRN which we assume to cost par and to pay Libor flat (ie with no margin) and which can be shown as follows:

Figure 6.7a: Par FRN paying Libor

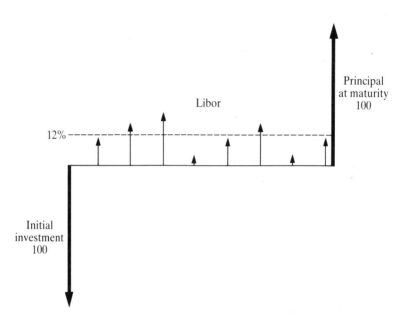

At the same time, the arranger sells an interest rate cap at 12 per cent to coincide with both the coupon fixing dates and the maturity of the FRN. The cap means that if Libor is higher on a fixing date, the arranger must pay the option buyer the difference between 12 per cent and the prevailing Libor. This can be shown diagramatically by referring to Figure 6.7b in which we assume that three of the coupon payments will be greater than 12 per cent (this is indicated by the dotted horizontal line) in Figure 6.7a. The cash flows on the cap therefore appear as follows:

Figure 6.7b: Sale of 12 per cent cap against Libor

The premium income received for the sale of the cap is used to purchase a fixed rate annuity which pays out on the coupon dates of the source FRN and matures on the last coupon payment date (or, in the case of a callable FRN, on the first call date).

The annuity can be illustrated as follows:

Figure 6.7c: Fixed rate annuity

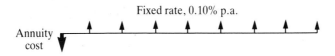

Combining the source FRN, interest rate cap contract and the annuity, the investor purchases a capped FRN which can be shown as follows:

Figure 6.7d: Resultant synthetic capped FRN

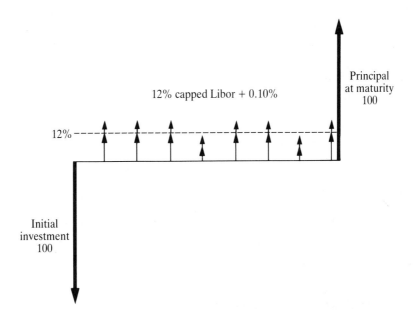

Note that the cap only comes into effect on the second, third and fifth coupon payment dates and that the FRN pays out a fixed maximum rate of the cap level on these occasions.

Callable FRN's Investors should be aware of the inadvisability of selling caps beyond the call date of callable FRNs. If interest rates rise substantially at the call date the issuer may be inclined to refinance the FRN issue in some other market. This would leave the investor exposed to the commitment to pay out on the cap he had sold without the expected higher Libor receipts from the

FRN. To compound the problem the cost of buying back the cap sold would have risen as the cap moved into the money (although this may be offset to some extent by time decay if the option had been sold some time ago.)

Setting the strike price on the cap contract sold If the FRN pays Libor plus a margin then the margin should be taken into account when setting the strike price on the cap sold. For example, if the FRN pays Libor plus 1/4 per cent and the cap is set at 12 per cent the investor will have achieved an *effective cap level* of 12 1/4 per cent.

FRN and cap rate setting basis Cap contracts, in common with most interest rate agreements, are slightly price sensitive to the interest rate fixing basis. Caps with six months' Libor setting are typically more valuable than one or three month settings due to the normal positive slope of the short end of the yield curve which reflects the time value of money.

Minimax floating rate notes

Minimax FRNs are similar to capped FRNs, in so far as they are limited to paying a maximum rate. They differ, however, in that they also define a minimum rate which the bond must always pay out, irrespective of prevailing market conditions, or level of Libor. In buying a Minimax FRN an investor effectively buys a bullet FRN, sells an interest rate cap contract and buys a interest rate floor contract. Each of these transactions is done with the FRN issuer, who may then sell off the cap he has purchased and buy back the floor he has sold in order to realise a gain and thereby reduce the true cost of issuing the FRN. The creation of a minimax FRN is the same as for a capped FRN, discussed above, with the addition of the purchase by the arranger of an interest rate floor contract.

The arranger buys a bullet FRN, which as before, may be sourced from the public FRN market or may be a synthetic FRN sourced from another fixed rate bond market.

Figure 6.8a: Par FRN paying Libor

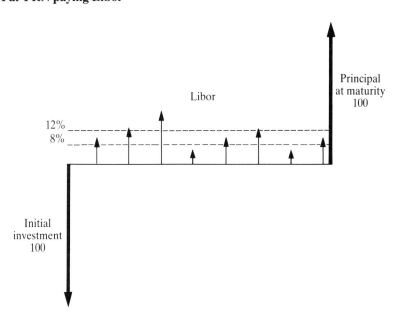

The arranger sells an interest rate cap contract with the cap payments being effected on the 2nd, 3rd and 5th coupons.

The arranger buys an interest rate floor contract which takes effect when coupons are below, for example, 8 per cent. The 8 per cent floor is hit on coupon numbers 4 and 7, and this is indicated by the floating rate coupon arrows falling short of the dotted line which represents 8 per cent in Figure 6.8a. The payments received by the arranger under the floor contract and the net premium paid to buy the floor are shown below:

Figure 6.8b: Sale of 12 per cent cap against Libor

Figure 6.8c: Purchase of 8 per cent floor against Libor

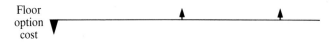

The net options premium, which we shall assume to be positive, is used to buy a small fixed rate annuity which is used by the arranger to enhance the margin over the funding base on the source FRN when rates are between the cap and floor levels.

The minimax FRN with all coupons being clearly within a narrow band set by the adjusted strike levels of the interest rate options is shown below:

Figure 6.8d: Resultant synthetic minimax FRN

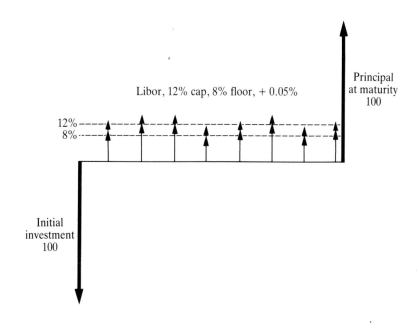

Exposure to changes in interest rate option values By both selling and buying interest rate option contracts, the investor has reduced his exposure to changes in the volatility of interest rates which are one of the primary determinants of option prices. Unlike the capped FRN, in which the investor has only sold an option and is therefore net short of option volatility, the buyer of a minimax FRN has a square position in option volatility and he therefore does not suffer a fall in the value of his asset if interest rates volatility increases.

However, the buyer of the minimax FRN does not benefit in the same way as the capped FRN holder from the time decay of being net short of options. This means that the value of the interest rate cap sold by the capped FRN holder will decay as expiry approaches (assuming that the cap level has not been reached). Consequently, the value of the secondary market price of the capped FRN can be expected to rise as maturity approaches. The minimax holder, however, finds that although the value of the cap sold falls (increasing the value of the minimax FRN), the value of the purchased floor also falls (decreasing the value of the minimax FRN) and if interest rates remain unchanged the two effects tend to cancel each other out (depending upon the exact strike levels of the cap and floor) with no net trend for the price of the minimax FRN as maturity approaches.

The cap and floor levels As discussed under the capped FRN, the strike levels on the option contract should also take into account the margin over the funding base on the source FRN. Remember that the margin is to be *added* to the cap level and *subtracted* from the floor level.

Step-up/step-down FRN

The step-up or step-down FRN is no more than an FRN which pays a margin which changes at specific times over the life of the bond. Changes in margin can be an extra complication for investors but can be suitable for issues in which the investor perceives the credit risk likely to change over time, and therefore requires a change in margin to reflect the change in risk. A few of these bonds were in fact issued but were without exception structured to benefit issuers rather than investors.

The step-up FRN is no more than a normal FRN combined with two annuities of the same maturity but different start dates, which when combined constitute the increasing margin. Issuers could use a positively sloping yield curve to disguise the fact that more margin at the tail end of the FRN's life was worth less to the investor in present value terms. Essentially, the issuer is arbitraging an observed difference between the reinvestment rate assumptions used by issuers and investors. Investors were persuaded to use money market yields (the short end of the yield curve) while issuers were using the bond market yield on a zero coupon basis. Investors used to floating rate money market instruments did not have suitable analytical tools to evaluate the combination of two fixed rate annuities contained within these new instruments and, although unsure of their true value, were persuaded by the notionally higher than normal margins. The secondary market price of these FRNs typically falls after issue date and does not recover until the higher margin approaches.

A step-down FRN is a normal FRN plus two annuities which start together but which end at different times. The secondary market price will stay high until the lower margin approaches, then will fall in value until it trades like a shorter maturity FRN with the lower margin.

Since both these structures are so simple, and of such marginal value to investors, no diagramatical analysis is needed.

Drop-lock FRNs

A drop-lock FRN is an FRN which pays a set margin over Libor until Libor falls to a predetermined level, in which case all future coupons remain at that level irrespective of the prevailing level of Libor. This transaction structure is yet another in which the investor sells the issuer an embedded option, in this case an option on an interest rate swap, a swaption. The investor has bought a normal FRN, and has sold the issuer the right to pay fixed rate and receive floating rate for an unknown length of time (except that the final maturity of the swaption is fixed by the maturity of the bond). The strike price on the option is the fixed rate that Libor must fall to before the option is automatically triggered. As interest rate swaps are priced off the treasury bond market plus a spread and the embedded swaption is based on Libor, the issuer has purchased an unusual swaption which may be difficult to value due to the yield curve risk between Libor and the appropriate maturity bond. However, this is usually beneficial to the issuer who, if the swaption is exercised, pays fixed rate at a much lower rate than a conventional swaption would allow.

Constructing a drop-lock FRN for an investor who thought that if interest rates fell they would fall a long way, and wanted to protect his portfolio by having a floating rate asset which would automatically become a fixed rate asset if interest rates fell below a specific level, the arranger first buys a normal FRN:

Figure 6.9a: Par FRN paying Libor

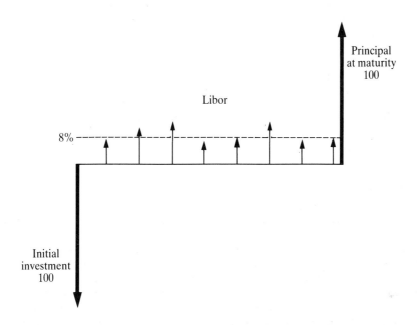

The arranger then sells a swaption with a strike price of 8 per cent against Libor for the same maturity as the source FRN. The swaption is represented by an interest rate swap which commences when the coupons on the FRN first fall below 8 per cent, which is indicated by the horizontal dotted line in Figure 6.9a.

Figure 6.9b: Sale of 8 per cent swaption against Libor

The premium received by the arranger for selling the swaption is used to buy a fixed rate annuity in order to enhance the margin payments as follows:

Figure 6.9c: Resultant synthetic drop-lock FRN

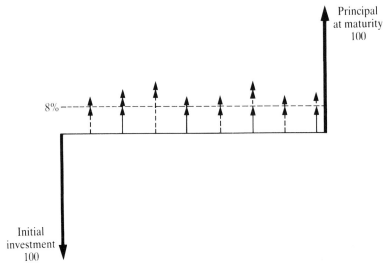

By combining the FRN, swaption and fixed rate annuity the investor has a high yielding FRN which converts to a fixed rate bond when Libor equals 8 per cent .

Setting the swaption strike level The swaption can be set against either Libor or against the return paid by the FRN in which case the strike level at which the swaption can be sold is lower by the margin on the FRN.

Currency and interest rate linked synthetics

First, we consider a floating rate bond created from a fixed rate bond in another currency. The cross currency synthetic FRN is a combination of fixed rate bond in currency A, and a currency and interest rate swap into currency B. This transaction is in widespread application in the market.

Fixed rate bond in currency A is purchased and can be represented as follows:

Figure 6.10a: Currency A fixed rate bond

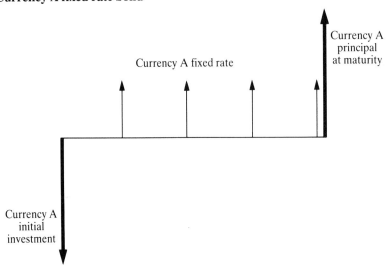

The currency swap of both principal (par forward exchange) and coupons (serial coupon swap) in which fixed rate payments are made in currency A and floating rate payments received in currency B is shown below:

Figure 6.10b: Fixed currency A to floating currency B swap

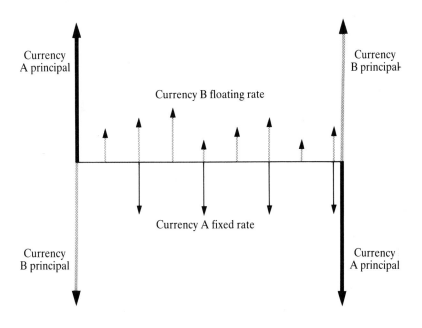

By netting all currency A cash flows from the bond and cross currency swap against each other the only remaining cash flows are principal and floating rate payments in currency B:

Figure 6.10c: Resultant synthetic currency B FRN

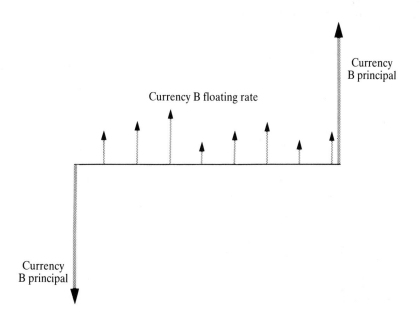

The purchased accrued interest on the fixed rate bond must be either funded through to payment, in which case the currency swap provider only accrues interest from the commencement of the swap, or it can be sold to the currency swap provider who will then receive the full year's coupon.

Capped floating rate bond

Our final example combines a cross currency synthetic FRN with the capped FRN and a currency option linked bond. We start by taking the completed cross currency synthetic FRN:

Figure 6.11a: Synthetic currency B FRN

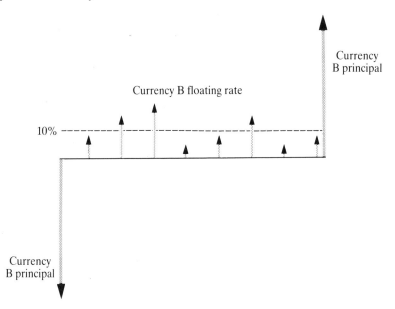

Next, the arranger sells a 10 per cent interest rate cap in currency B, which is indicated by payments which are made when the floating rate coupons from the cross currency FRN are greater than the horizontal line drawn at 10 per cent in Figure 6.11a.

Figure 6.11b: Sale of 10 per cent currency B cap against Libor

The arranger then sells a currency option for the issuer to be allowed to repay the maturing bond in currency C. (If the option were to be back into the source bond's original currency, in this case A, the arranger would not transact the currency principal swap, but would rather sell an option for the issuer to repay in currency B at maturity, and would perform a spot exchange selling A and buying B. The two option premiums are combined to purchase a fixed rate currency B annuity in order to increase the margin over the funding base:

104

Figure 6.11c: Sale of currency B/currency C option

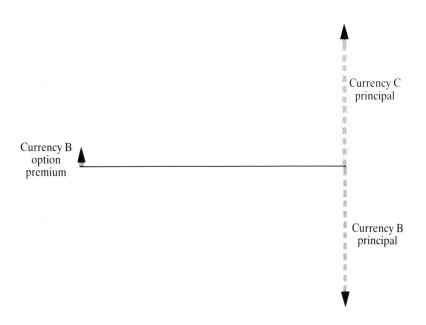

Figure 6.11d: Purchase of currency B annuity

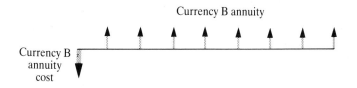

The net instrument appears as follows:

Figure 6.11e: Resultant synthetic currency B capped, variable redemption FRN

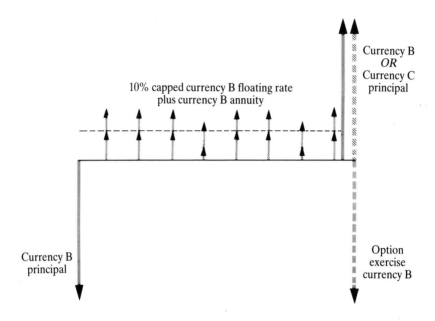

Conclusion

In this chapter we have shown that many complex structures can be achieved using the concepts of synthetic securities and the range of hedge techniques which are available today. We have not provided an exhaustive list of options, as the possibilities are almost boundless. However, we hope that we have encouraged investors to be more adventurous in applying these techniques to their portfolio holdings.

CHAPTER 7
Case study: floating rate notes; repackaging and innovation

Floating rate notes

Although there are numerous formulae for valuing floating rate notes (FRNs) there is no valuation method which guarantees the return over life for an FRN trading at a price other than par (100), or which is accurate if the investor is not match funding.

The following formula is widely used to achieve the discount (or 'true') margin for FRNs.

$$DM = \frac{100 - ((CP + A) + ((L + QM) \times d/360) - C)}{Life}$$

where:
— Discount margin = DM
— Clean bond price = CP
— Accrued interest = A
— Libor to the next coupon date = L
— Quoted margin over Libor = QM
— Days from settlement to next coupon = d
— Current coupon (including margin) = C
— Life = Life (in decimalised years) from settlement date to maturity

Although the formula does not exactly calculate true margin, as it still requires the assumption that future Libor rates will be the same as current rates (and it is therefore an adjusted simple margin formula), it is in widespread use by FRN traders and investors.

Changes in interest rates have three effects on the valuation of FRNs:
— discounting the spread over Libor over the life of the bond;
— discounting the capital gain or loss resulting from buying the bond at a price other than par at maturity;
— discounting the difference between funding the purchase price and receiving coupons on the notional amount.

The calculation assumes a constant Libor rate which is used to discount the margin over Libor for the remaining life, to present value the capital gain or loss at final maturity and both to calculate and discount the value of the Libor plus margin on the difference between notional and cost 'free Libor'. Although this rate is taken to be the current Libor it clearly exposes the investor to substantial interest rate risk as any changes in Libor expose the investor to losses resulting from changing the rate at which the margin, capital gain/loss and 'free Libor' are discounted.

This risk is reduced if the investor is match funding the investment (borowing funds on the same basis ie Libor and on the same rollover dates as the FRN); this reduces the risk of a variation in return due to changes in Libor as the investor has an equal and offsetting change in his funding. However, even the match-funded investor continues to be exposed to the effect of changes in the discount rate on the capital gain/loss at maturity, and in a positively sloping yield curve environment, investors are underestimating the size of this effect by using an artificially low discount rate (the current Libor).

This effect is small for bonds trading close to par as the size of the forward capital gain/loss is small in future value terms and hence extremely small in present value terms. For example, the effect on the price of an FRN when bonds are trading in the region of 99 to 101 is approximately one basis point, so changes in the discount rate used will have a correspondingly small effect. However, for bonds trading at 90 a 1 per cent change in the discount rate from 9 per cent to 10 per cent will change the price by as much as a result of the effect on capital alone. Similarly, for bonds trading at deep discounts a rise in interest rates may cause the beneficial effect of the 'free Libor' to be much larger than the negative effect of discounting the coupons and capital gain at maturity at an increased discount rate.

There are additional problems caused by buying FRNs at a discount to par, as the amount of the portfolio will not neccesarily equal the round amounts lenders normally choose to lend. This has the effect of making accurate match funding extremely difficult, and makes the assumption used in the FRN valuation formula, that all FRNs will be match funded, invalid.

Investors are aware of these limitations in the valuation technique and are increasingly demanding both a higher level of return to compensate for these risks and an even cash flow which can be relied upon over the entire life of the FRN. In addition, investors have become dissatisfied with the extreme price volatility of all types of FRNs which has bedevilled the market since the collapse of the perpetual FRN market in early 1987. This has resulted in investors being obliged to account for revaluation losses when their objective was to hold dated FRNs through to maturity.

Repackaging

By restructuring FRNs which are available in the public market at prices other than par (in some cases at substantial discounts) into par bonds the investor avoids exposure to changes in interest rates because he knows in advance what his cash flows will be. Furthermore, in the absence of major changes in the credit worthiness of the original issuer, the investor can rightfully revalue the restructured FRN at par, instead of having to revalue at the prevailing market price.

To transform discount FRNs purchased in the secondary FRN market the arranger must reinvest the discount and use the proceeds to enhance the margin paid by the original bonds. The majority of retructured FRNs are those in which the underlying bond is purchased at a discount and the synthetic package sold at par. The cash balance held by the arranger is reinvested to enhance the coupon payments made to the investor. The normal, positively sloping, yield curve environment means that investments in longer instruments generate a greater return than those in short-term money market deposits. However, the arranger must manage the greater volatality of these longer instruments. By investing the cash balance in annuities or treasury strips the return to the investor can be enhanced compared with short-term Libor, but this is only possible in sizeable amounts. Thus, by pooling the cash amounts it is possible to obtain the best yields on the hedging instruments.

In order to repackage an FRN, the arranger holds the underlying bond in safe custody while the investor remains the beneficial owner. The arranging bank collects the coupons direct from the bond, and manages the gaps between uneven cashflows received and even cashflows paid out to the investor. This relieves the investor of much tedious paper work as he merely receives Libor plus the agreed margin.

Additionally, repackaged FRNs can be tailored to suit an individual investor's needs by, for example, matching the exact coupon payment dates, thereby giving the investor more freedom in arranging his financing.

Innovation in the FRN market

When yields on existing FRNs were declining during 1985 and 1986, investment bankers looked for new ways to create low-cost financing in order to win mandates from issuers. At the same time, investors looked for ways to increase their returns.

Capped floating rate note

In September 1986 issuers, ever ready to take advantage of any arbitrage window-opening, began to issue *capped FRNs*. These paid on average Libor plus 25 basis points, compared with typical margins at the time of Libor plus ⅛ per cent to ¹⁄₁₆ per cent , thus satisfying investors' needs for greater yield, but limited the investor to a maximum return of around 13 per cent . The issuer had effectively purchased a 13 per cent cap from the investor and had compensated the investor by increasing the margin over Libor. The issuer was able to sell the 13 per cent cap in the options market for a greater value than the cost of the additional margin paid to investors and thereby reduce his effective cost of raising funds to below Libor. See Chapter 6 for a full description of capped FRNs.

This innovation was popular for a short period but when interest rates rose and it seemed that the cap level might be reached investor interest waned very quickly and the market in capped FRNs is now quite illiquid. These bonds can be retructured either by removing the interest rate cap and selling the FRN as an uncapped (ie normal), bullet FRN, or by removing the cap and replacing it with one which is more acceptable in prevailing market conditions. To be succesful with either strategy the arranger must still achieve a good spread over Libor.

Mis-match floating rate note

Similarly, at a time when there was a steep yield curve in short-term interest rates, the *mis-match* FRN was in vogue. This has the coupon fixing based on a different term than the interest is actually paid on. For example, the coupon might be six months Libor fixed monthly and paid semi-annually. The investor gained by the difference between one and six month rates as he could now match fund using one month Libor rollovers on which he was accruing six months' Libor. The issuer benefited by a reduction in the spread against Libor. Once again, investor interest fell rapidly as the yield curve flattened and the cost of rolling over one month funding and accruing the cost of funding monthly against receiving the coupon semi-annually was factored into the yield calculation leading to a lower, or in some cases negative, return against Libor.

Sophisticated hedging techniques enable some arrangers to restructure these bonds into conventional FRNs to provide straight six months' Libor plus margin income.

Minimax floating rate note

Another short-lived innovation was the *minimax* FRN. These bonds have a minimum coupon of around 10 per cent and a maximum of around 11.5 per cent. The investor has effectively purchased a minimum rate, or 'floor', at 10 per cent and has sold a maximum rate, or cap, of 11.5 per cent and is compensated for transacting these options with the issuer by a higher margin over Libor. The issuer benefits in the same manner as discussed under the capped FRNs above, by selling the covering the options bought and sold at a profit with the options market. Only three issues were launched before investor demand was satiated and these are now extremely illiquid. See Chapter 6 for a full description of Minimax FRNs.

There are several other examples of innovation in the FRN market such as *step up/step down* FRNs, *drop-lock* FRNs and *issuers option to select fixing period*, each of which also suffered from mark-downs and illiquidty.

Alternative innovations

The concept of linking the FRN with a money market option is not neccesarily a bad one, and may create securities which have particular appeal to certain types of investor. However, the way in which these bonds have performed in the primary and secondary markets illustrates the problems which face all investors in new types of instrument, as follows:

— The first concern is that the pricing at new issue is usually biased heavily in favour of the issuer — in other words, the investor gets a raw deal;

— this is compounded by the risk premium which the lead manager feels obliged to charge, both to compensate for the risk of bringing a new and untried structure to the market and as a reward for innovation;

— in the secondary market the bonds quickly fall to a 'fair value level' resulting in revaluation losses for the investor; but

— worse still, all liquidity dries up, leaving the investor with a loss-making position in an instrument with a highly defined risk profile and no way to liquidate the holding at other than a 'fire-sale' price.

If, by contrast, investors who explicitly wanted to hold capped or mis-match or mini-max or any other type of non- standard FRNs had arranged for their desired instrument to be made especially for them by an arranging bank, none of these problems would have been encountered.

This is because:

— The pricing would be at the level appropriate for the combination of source instrument, hedge technique/money market option and the cost to the arranger of managing any residual risk;

— the investor has no additional risk premium to bear as the arranger knows that he will not be obliged to hold a risky position in inventory for any length of time;

— as the restructured instrument (or synthetic FRN, as the source bond may not be an FRN and may therefore require some type of swap) is bought at a fair value level the investor will not be exposed to substantial negative price movements which are so typical immediately after a public issue;

— finally, liquidity is maintained as the arranger is always able to bid for the restructured package valued against either the market bid for each of the components or demand from investors wanting similar products.

Conclusion

The restructured floating rate note takes advantage of market pricing anomalies and frequently uses the less popular instruments which have fallen below their 'fair value level' in order to create new instruments. These restructured FRNs satisfy investor demand for both regular high yielding floating rate assets and for highly specific types of investment instrument.

The primary market no longer has a monopoly on innovation as investors can now use the principles of synthetic securities to repackage instruments to meet their own specific investment requirements, rather than invest in the issues created for the expediency of the issuer.

CHAPTER 8
Effects on the bond and swap markets

Introduction

The widespread application of the techniques reviewed in this book has had a significant effect on each of three separate markets:

— the Eurobond market;

— the interest rate and, to a lesser extent, the currency swap market; and

— the market for substitute investments such as publically issued FRNs and syndicated loans.

This chapter considers each in turn.

Eurobond market

The effects of mass production of synthetic securities from mid 1985 onwards has resulted in approximately US$ 80-85 billion of fixed coupon, principally US dollar denominated, Eurobonds (and some domestic and other currency bonds) being taken out of the market. During this period there has been approximately US$ 370 billion of US dollar new issues, US$ 120 billion of redemptions and an estimated US$ 50 billion of repurchases by issuers in the fixed income bond market. Whichever way this information is analysed the same conclusion is reached, the US dollar-denominated part of the fixed income Euromarkets, in which most synthesising has been carried out is shrinking in both absolute and in real (inflation and currency adjusted) terms. The effects of synthesising have accelerated this trend.

Most restructured bonds are sold to an investor who would typically fall outside the domain of the Euromarkets, whose intention is to hold the restructured instrument until its maturity. This results in reduced supply of each of those issues which have been subject to restructuring activity, with a corresponding decline in traders' willingness to make active markets in those bonds. (Traders adopt the logical stance of being unwilling to 'go short' bonds they do not hold in inventory as they risk the possibility of not being able to source replacement bonds from the market.) It is the price at which different bonds trade which makes them candidates for swapping or not.

Once a particular issue becomes swappable it tends to become rapidly illiquid, in so far as it no longer has many active market makers and cannot therefore be traded in large size. The process of synthesising has the effect of polarising all issues into those which remain liquid as they have not been swapped and those which have been partly swapped and which therefore become illiquid. There is an argument that only bonds which are already illiquid become candidates for the swap process rather than swapping making the bonds illiquid. In practice, the order of the two effects is indistinguishable and anyway is of little consequence as the same conclusion remains: the market becomes polarised into liquid and illiquid securities.

This polarisation of the bond market into actively traded, liquid securities and securities in which there is little supply, as most of the bonds are locked away in investors' portfolios linked to swaps, is regarded by many as 'a bad thing' for the bond market overall. We disagree. Prior to the development of a widespread market for synthetic securities there was no minimum level at which any particular bond could trade. The market value of each bond was at the discretion of the market makers who balanced supply and demand. Investors in issues which were particularly unpopular, and unsuccessful, realised large losses. Synthetic securities introduced an *objective measure of value*, the value at which restructured instruments could be placed with investors in any of the markets linked through the interest rate or currency swap. This allowed investment bankers to buy any securities trading at or below the objective measure of value resulting in even the least popular issues trading *to value*. This process limits the potential losses of fixed income investors to the level at which the swap becomes possible, thereby providing liquidity for the securities for which previously no bid could be obtained. The provision of liquidity for this part of the fixed income markets is more beneficial than the loss of trading liquidity due to the reduction in supply for those issues which have been swapped.

Life cycle of a Eurobond

One of the best ways to illustrate this is by comparing three possible alternative lives of the same bond issued in the Euromarkets:

— successful issue

— typical issue

— unsuccessful issue

Successful issue

Figure 8.1 illustrates the spread over risk-free securities at which a corporate Eurobond is issued (far left of figure) and at which the bonds trades over its life. By graphing spread rather than price we are able to view the relative value of the corporate bond against the government bond without any distortions caused by changes in interest rates, which would change the value of both bonds together. This approach separates changes in *relative value* from changes in *absolute value*. The *spread* represents compensation to the investor for the combination of *credit risk*, as a result of buying corporate rather than goverment paper, and *liquidity risk*, for investing in a non-government market in which liquidity is not assured. As the time to maturity reduces so does the spread, as investors demand less compensation over and above risk-free securities for the reduced period of uncertainties regarding credit and liquidity, and so the graphed line moves down to the right.

Figure 8.1: Life cycle of a Eurobond: Successful issue

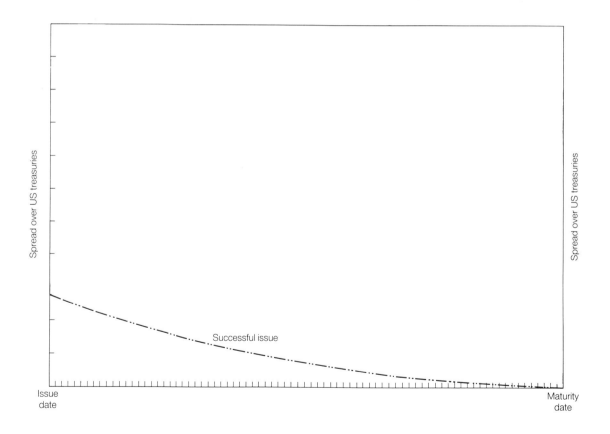

Typical issue

Our second bond (see Figure 8.2) was issued at the same spread but due to poor primary market syndication, or an absence of interest from investors, fell to a wider spread during the period immediately after the launch date. This phenomena has been a frequent occurence in the highly competitive markets over the past few years as investment banks have attempted to buy share in the new issue market by offering issuers terms which their syndicate or distribution skills could not match. The spread over risk-free securities which any bond trades to is a combination of credit and liquidity premium. An absence of liquidity in the secondary market, as a result of the lead manager being unsuccesful in forming a strong syndicate group, or in persuading a number of other market makers to take up the issue, will generally result in investors demanding a higher liquidity premium in compensation. The practice favours issuers at the expense of both investors and the issuing house (which usually accepts the implicit subsidy it is paying the issuer). As in our previous example, once the issue has been succesfully placed the spread falls as maturity approaches.

Figure 8.2: Life cycle of a Eurobond: Typical issue

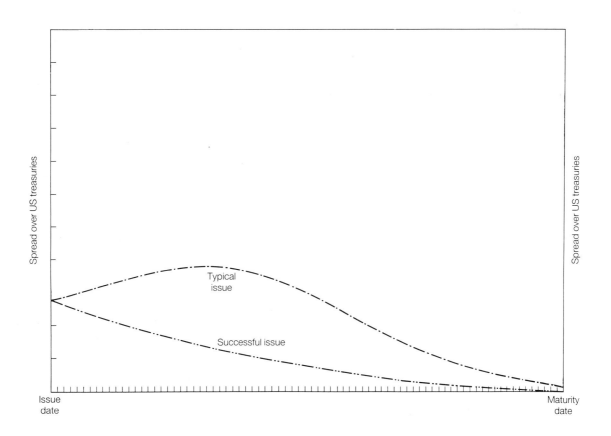

Unsuccessful issue

Our third example (see Figure 8.3) is of a bond which met with significant investor resistance and which would have fallen in value to a very substantial spread premium over risk-free securities compared with issues which were launched successfully (Figure 8.1) or which only slipped a small amount after issue (Figure 8.2). This is shown by the exaggerated bulge in the spread immediately after issue which does not recover to usual levels until almost maturity.

Figure 8.3: Life cycle of a Eurobond: Unsuccessful issue

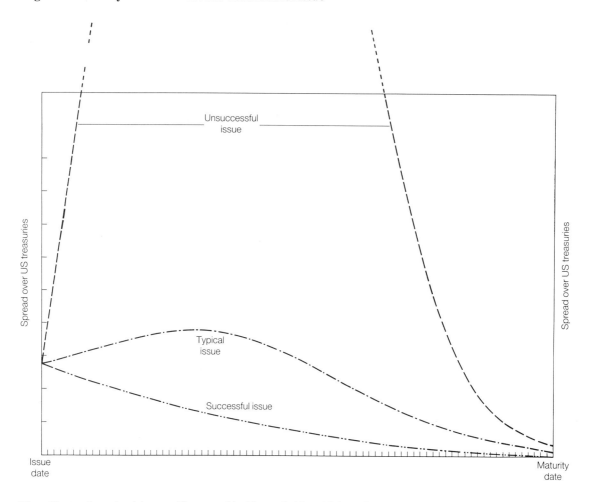

The effects of synthesising are illustrated in Figure 8.4 in which we have added a new line representing the *objective value* or swap curve at which spread bonds can be transformed into another market and sold to investors. The different type of hedge technique used is indicated along the bottom axis; initially swaps, followed by floating rate assets (FRAs) and then money market hedges.

Figure 8.4: Life cycle of a Eurobond: The value line

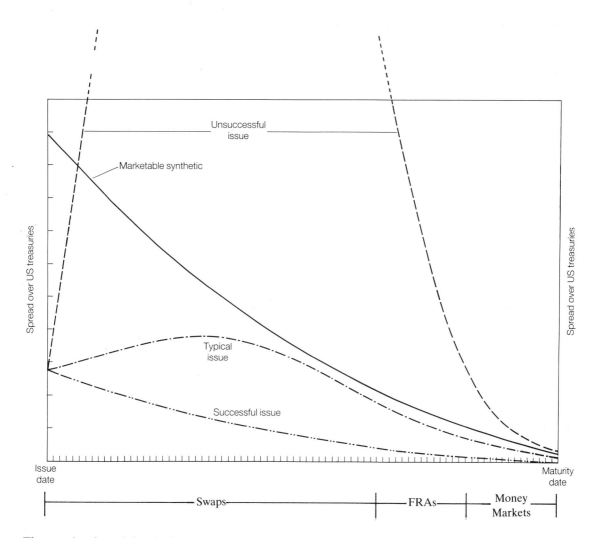

The result of applying hedge techniques to the least succesful bond is to improve dramatically its performance in the secondary market. The bond now trades just on, or below, the hedge *value line* as every time the bond becomes cheaper than this line, restructurers are willing buyers and their activity succeeds in bidding the price back up again, substantially reducing investors' possibility of making losses. This is illustrated in Figure 8.5.

Figure 8.5: Life cycle of a Eurobond: The effects of synthesising

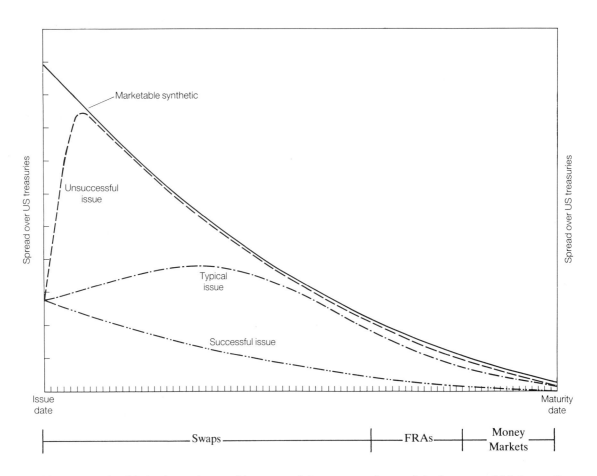

This process should also be understood in terms of the swap market, as it is the swap which is usually responsible for both transactions — the new issue and the subsequent restructuring. Taking our example to be a straightforward fixed rate US dollar bond, it is likely that the issue was swapped into sub-Libor floating rate funds at the issue date. This swap would have been executed at the bid side of the swap (ie the rate at which the swap provider bids for fixed rate funds and pays the issuer a fixed rate which the issuer in turn uses to service the issue coupon). The restructure of the fixed rate bond into a floating rate asset requires a swap priced off the offered side of the swap (ie the rate at which the swap provider offers fixed rate funds and receives the fixed rate which the investor provides from the fixed rate bond). So, the bid and offered swap spreads are a fundamental determinant of the spread levels of both new issues and subsequent restructurings.

Swaps market

The active use of the swaps market by restructurers has had a dramatic effect on the swap market in terms of swap volumes, pricing and swap availability or liquidity.

Swap volumes

At least US$ 60-65 billion of interest rate and perhaps US$ 20-25 billion of currency swaps have been transacted solely for the purpose of creating packages of synthetic securities since mid 1985. Although this does not represent more than an estimated 15 per cent of the swap market, it is incremental volume most of which is believed to have been transacted at the swap market makers' price, unlike much of the swap volume associated with the new issues market in which many swaps are largely a cross-subsidy of the new issue.

Swap pricing

Bid-offered spreads in US dollar interest rate swaps were typically 20 basis points wide at the end of 1985 and, on occasion, only one side of the price could be said to really *work*. With the increase in swap volume and the dramatic increase in the frequency of transactions (higher volumes and smaller transaction size typify most synthetics transactions) swaps market makers were able to get a regular and accurate fix on their pricing from the restructurers. The knowledge that deals could be executed almost continuously on their own price encouraged swaps warehouse managers to update prices constantly with a view to attracting synthetic securities business, allowing them to earn the bid-offered spread.

The other important feature of synthetic activity from the perspective of the swaps warehouse manager was that synthetics deals were the natural offset to swaps done for issuers in conjunction with a new issue (in which the issuer issues a fixed rate bond and pays floating rate to the warehouse, receiving fixed rate which is used to service the coupon payments on the fixed rate bond leaving the issuer with a net floating rate borrowing). Warehouse managers could use synthetics to run down the large swap positions which were taken on in conjunction with new issues, without having to offset any part of the position with competitors at unfavourable prices.

All of these factors encouraged swaps warehouses to reduce their bid-offered spreads to the level of 10 to 15 basis points seen today. This, however, may be a passing phenomenon as the effect of the regulators establishing capital requirements for swaps is more likely to cause bankers to increase spreads, take on more risky transactions or devise some alternative method for transacting so as to avoid the capital requirement.

Market for substitute instruments

Public FRN market

Most synthetic securities are made in the form of US dollar floating rate notes, and it is the effect on the FRN market of creating synthetic securities which is most interesting. Other types of synthetic security have been produced in significant quantities but not in sufficient size so as to have a material effect on the substitute market.

The major collapse in the FRN market in early 1987 was due to the fact that investors in perpetual FRNs realised that these instruments were an equity risk (many do not pay interest if a dividend is not paid by the issuer) but only paid a money market return. We do not claim that the effects of creating synthetic securities had any effect on this particular crisis. Nevertheless, since the perpetual FRN collapse, the dated FRN issues (those with a specified maturity) have traded at very large discounts to the levels seen previously.

The reasons for this are a widespread loss of confidence in the active trading of money market instruments which offer little potential for gain but, on occasion, can provide investors with very large revaluation losses. In addition, investors found the FRN market increasingly illiquid as the decline in trading volumes of FRNs caused many market makers, who require volume to earn trading profit, to withdraw from the market. This decline in liquidity, combined with a realisation that synthetic securities had become widely available at yield levels substantially in excess of those on offer in the public FRN market, and that synthetics were likely to continue to be a long-term factor in the market, resulted in investors largely abandoning the public FRN market. Without this third factor of more supply at better yields, the FRN market would have experienced a stronger recovery than it has achieved to date.

Syndicated loan market

Synthetic FRNs are similar to participations in syndicated loans, and the investor groups overlap extensively. It is not surprising therefore that the synthetic FRN has developed whereas the syndicated loan loan market has been growing only slowly. One feature of the linkage between these two markets is the behaviour of some middle ranking corporate borrowers. These borrowers, who could access the syndicated loan market, but who prefer not to do so for reasons of prestige, issue fixed rate bonds of the type typically only issued by top quality corporates. The borrower swaps the fixed rate proceeds of the issue for floating rate funds at an all-in cost similar to that which would have been obtained from a syndicated loan. The fixed rate bonds are sold in the market to the *same* banks which would make up the syndicate. These banks then execute interest rate swaps against the bonds in order to create synthetic floating rate assets. The result is the same as if the borrower had raised funds in the syndicated loan market, but the mechanism is more complex, involving two opposite interest rate swaps and a fixed rate bond issue.

Conclusion

Synthetic securities have had a significant effect on the bond, swap and substitute instrument markets.

In the bond market, large amounts of bonds have been taken out of circulation, resulting in the *polarisation* of the fixed income market into liquid and illiquid securities. Bonds now *trade to value* as a result of the application of the arbitrage techniques used by synthetics. Also, synthetics provide new issue managers with a low cost *exit strategy* for issues which do not have sufficient investor demand. Finally, and perhaps most importantly, synthetics have helped to keep the bond markets active during a time of volatile and rising interest rates by providing access to a new type of investor, the commercial bank portfolio manager.

Swaps volumes have increased and the market's familiarity with swap techniques has grown outside those traditionally associated with issuer driven, liability swaps. At the same time, the availability of swaps against assets has provided swap warehouse managers with almost constant access to one side of a swap allowing them both to quote more aggresively for offsetting liabilty swaps and to unwind adverse positions with greater ease than previously.

Synthetic securities have competed effectively for investor attention in the market for substitute instruments. Public FRNs have become unfashionable as investors became disillusioned with high price volatilty and realised that the market's apparent liquidity was not sufficient to survive a sustained sell-off. Syndicated loans suffered as synthetics were able to service both bank and securities investors from the same underlying instrument.

This final point illustrates the most fundamental reason behind the success of synthetic securities at the expense of other instruments and markets. The synthetic security is able to satisfy the needs of all types of investor, whereas traditional investment instruments are typically highly focused on small sub-groups within the investor community.

SECTION 4

Legal and tax

Section 4 covers the legal, tax and accounting issues which face producers of synthetic securities. It is structured in two parts:

Chapter 9 covers the various legal structures used to evidence synthetic securities transactions, and was written jointly by Chris Wyman and Robert Palache, both partners in the banking department at Clifford Chance.

Chapter 10 examines the tax and accounting implications for investors and was written by Emma Lubbock of Price Waterhouse, and Richard Kilsby of Charterhouse Bank Ltd.

There is no explicit section on regulatory issues as there are no regulations which apply specifically to synthetics, and such regulations which do apply are generic to the markets for the underlying source instrument and hedge techniques.

CHAPTER 9
Legal aspects of synthetic securities

by
Chris Wyman and Robert Palache, Clifford Chance

Introduction

The diversification of the swap market from a concentration on *liability* swaps to encompass asset swaps has resulted in the need for the development of new legal instruments. As the asset swap market has become more sophisticated, so the requirement has arisen for more complex legal documentation to convey adequately the intentions of the parties and address the wide ranging legal implications of such contracts.

Generally, the term synthetic security has been employed to designate asset swaps. This usage can, however, lead to confusion, as a range of instruments tend to be bundled together under this title which, although they have similar characteristics, nevertheless display a number of distinctive features.

In an attempt to make the terms more precise, such instruments will be discussed here under three separate titles — asset swaps, collateralised asset swaps and synthetic securities. The instruments designated as such reflect a clear development both chronologically in terms of the development of the swap market and in terms of complexity. This process of growing sophistication is illustrated in Figures 9.1a-c.

Figure 9.1a: Asset Swap

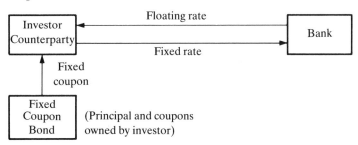

Figure 9.1b: Collateralised Asset Swap

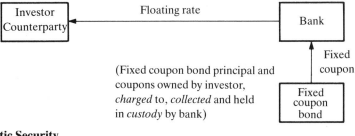

Figure 9.1c: Synthetic Security

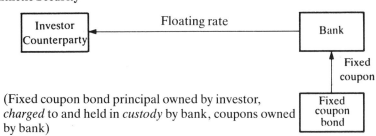

Asset swaps

While from a commercial point of view, the existence of the bond and the yield which it bears is the rationale behind an asset swap; from a legal viewpoint, the asset is incidental to the contract. The exposure of the bank is to the counterparty and therefore it is against the counterparty that the bank must seek fulfilment of any obligations under the asset swap contract. An asset swap contract therefore reveals no significant differences from the standard liability swap, and the legal issues involved do not differ significantly.

Collateralised asset swaps

It is clear that with an asset swap, where an asset underlies the contract, there is an opportunity for collateralisation of the swap which is not so readily available in the case of a liability swap. As a result, the practice has developed for banks to take a charge over the bond (principal and coupons) which the counterparty is using to generate the payments it is obliged to make under the asset swap. The bank thus has security for its risk against the counterparty which it does not have in the case of the standard asset swap.

The legal issues involved in taking such a charge are discussed below in relation to synthetic securities. There are no significant distinctions to be made from a legal point of view between a collateralised asset swaps and a collateralised liability swap. The bank still looks to the counterparty as the obligor, and the terms of the contract must be drawn to protect the interests of the bank and the counterparty on this basis.

Synthetic securities

In a synthetic security, the bank sells the principal only of a bond to the counterparty over which it takes a charge. This charge gives the bank security against un-winding costs on default. The bank retains ownership of the coupons against payment of which it makes payments to the counterparty.

The development of an instrument which embodies this procedure reflects a qualitative development from the collateralised asset swap and can be accurately analysed as a synthetic floating rate note. There are a number of advantages to both parties in entering into a synthetic security rather than a collateralised asset swap, some of which will become clear from the following discussion.

The rest of this chapter will be devoted to a discussion of the legal issues involved in a synthetic securities programme as this is the most sophisticated of the asset swap instruments and the only one in the asset swap market which differs significantly from the liability swap from a legal point of view. The legal issues will be discussed as these relate to English law, with brief references to particular legal problems which arise in other jurisdictions.

Master Agreement

The terms and conditions of an agreement for sale of a synthetic security are of some complexity. However, the commercial realities existing in the market for such securities dictate tight time schedules. Because of the time factor, it is undesirable to introduce a complex legal document at the point when a deal is being struck. The practice has therefore arisen, as with other instruments in the swap market, for banks to enter into *master agreements* with prospective counterparties. Such an agreement will set out the standard terms and conditions upon which the bank will enter into synthetic securities transactions with a counterparty. Thereafter, the terms and conditions of such master agreement can be imported into each synthetic securities transaction entered into between the bank and that counterparty. A contract can then be concluded by telephone, normally followed by a confirmatory telex.

The Bank's security

By means of the synthetic security, the bank makes payment primarily against the coupons which it owns. As security for the obligations of the counterparty under the contract, and for the costs of unwinding on default by the counterparty, the bank looks primarily to the bond principal.

To make such an arrangement effective against the counterparty, specific provisions must be incorporated in the master agreement, firstly to provide for a first, fixed charge over the bond in favour of the bank and, secondly, to ensure that the proceeds of the bond on redemption are available in the first instance to satisfy any obligations owing to the bank under the security. Clearly it will be necessary in each case to ensure that the security created is effective against the counterparty under the law of its own jurisdiction.

Charge over bonds

After the bonds have been purchased by a counterparty, the bank holds them on behalf of the customer during the period of the synthetic securities transaction. The bank protects itself against the counterparty's contingent liability for the bank's losses on an unwinding of the synthetic security by taking a charge over the bonds.

The question arises as to whether the charge thus created would be registrable under section 395 of the 1985 Companies Act. For the charge to be registrable, the security would need to amount to either a charge over a book debt of the counterparty or a floating charge over the counterparty's assets.

While there is a body of opinion which holds that securities may constitute book debts of the beneficial owner, on balance, the general view would appear to be that it is unlikely that the charge would be regarded as constituting a charge over the book debt of the counterparty. It would not therefore be registerable by operation of section 396(e) of the 1985 Act.

On the other hand, the security over the bonds cannot be regarded as constituting a floating charge because a charge attaches to specific bonds on the occasion of entering into each synthetic securities contract. This conclusion is not affected by the fact that, in the relevant clause in the master agreement, the counterparty purports to grant a charge before the subject of the charge can be specified. The master agreement cannot stand on its own. Its terms are only effective when imported into each individual synthetic securities contract. Accordingly, when the clause creating the charge in the master agreement is rendered effective, the subject of the charge will be able to be identified with precision.

Negative pledges

The danger of contravening a negative pledge which has been previously granted by the counterparty in favour of a third party must always be borne in mind when constituting such a charge. Such a contravention could well render the counterparty in default under the contract which contained such a covenant. The consequences may not stop at this point, for an act of default may well trigger cross-default provisions in other agreements to which the counterparty is a party, resulting in the other parties thereto being entitled to terminate and claim any losses arising out of the counterparty's default.

For the bank's part, if it could be shown to have concluded the contract in the knowledge of the counterparty's negative pledge, there is the possibility that the bank's charge might be set aside by the courts at the instance of the beneficiary of the negative pledge, on its being liable in tort inducing breach of contract. The bank might, in that event, have to bear any losses incurred by the beneficiary of such a negative pledge resulting from the breach.

In addition, there is the possibility that the whole synthetic securities contract might be held to be void as a consequence of the illegality involved as a result of its being concluded deliberately in contravention of an existing pledge.

The bank will be protected against such dire consequences, in the first instance, by the inclusion in the master agreement of a warranty by the counterparty that its execution of the relevant synthetic securities contract will not violate any existing agreements. Such a warranty, as with all of the terms in the master agreement, should be drawn so as to ensure that it is repeated on entering each synthetic securities contract.

The possibility of breach of a negative pledge, however, is increased due to the fact that the date of execution of the master agreement, when the counterparty may be expected to be most acutely aware of its obligations thereunder, is of no relevance in connection with the creation of charges. The first charge against the counterparty may be created some time after execution of the master agreement and subsequent charges may be created thereafter, all by means of a contract concluded by a telephone conversation.

There is always the possibility, therefore, that a counterparty may be entering into a contract in breach of a negative pledge and the question arises as to what additional precautions, if any, the bank should take. It would appear that there is no general duty on the bank actively to inquire about the existence of prior contracts containing such provisions.[1] Nevertheless, it should be remembered that the bank may be regarded as having received constructive notice, at least of public documents, which certainly includes the information contained in the Register of Charges.[2] There is no clear authority, however, defining the full range of documents which will be regarded as providing constructive notice.[3]

It is another question whether, having received notice of a document which might contain a negative pledge, the bank is under an obligation to investigate the terms of that document to ascertain if it does in fact contain such provisions. It would appear unlikely that the bank will be found liable merely because it must have known that the counterparty had a contract of some kind or other with another party and that the synthetic securities contract might result in its breach.[4]

Cash account

On the redemption of the bond, the master agreement usually provides for cash received to be paid to the credit of an account in the name of the counterparty on the bank's books: the bank is given the right to apply any credit balances in satisfaction of any sums owing by the counterparty. Such an arrangement does not amount to a simple right of retention in favour of the bank pending the fulfilment of a condition as is the case in the classic flawed asset arrangement. Rather, it constitutes a right of retention together with a right of set-off.

The case of Charge-card lends support to the view that a bank's rights, in respect of accounts maintained with it, both of retention and set-off do not constitute a charge. The reasoning for this is that a charge in favour of a debtor over his own indebtedness is conceptionally impossible. If there is no charge, then the question of registrability under statute does not even arise.

It cannot be assumed, however, that the decision in Charge-card has conclusively determined this complex issue. Nevertheless, even if the bank's rights of set-off and retention are subsequently identified as a charge, in order for such a charge to be registrable it must fall within the definition of a book debt for the purposes of section 396(e) of the Companies Act 1985. There is at present some uncertainty as to whether the courts would regard such rights of a bank as falling within this definition. The recent case of Re Brightlife Ltd, though not directly in point, may land some weight to the view that such rights do not fall within this definition.

Notwithstanding these much debated points, in a synthetic securities contract as it has been described here, the rights which the bank has over the cash account do not constitute more than a contractual set-off which parallels the mandatory set-off on bankruptcy. As such would be difficult to imply that the parties intended to create a charge, nor is there a concern that the contractual terms might be identified as purporting to alter and *pari passu* principle and as such subject to being declared void on the bankruptcy of the counter party, because the statutory obligation to set-off would then arise. In those circumstances, it is not unreasonable to expect that the bank's rights over the cash account in a synthetic securities contract will not be registrable.

Bond clearing systems

The bonds traded in a synthetic securities contract will almost always be held by one of the principal bond clearing systems, Euro-clear and Cedel. This gives rise to a number of important issues in assessing the effectiveness of the securities taken by the bank over the bond. Such issues are themselves dependant on the answers to broader questions not least of relationships between participants, each of the bond clearing systems and the banks who act as depositories for the clearing systems. A full analysis of these relationships is a prerequisite for establishing the rights in relation to the bond lodged in a clearance system from the point of view of the participant (the bank), the counterparty and third parties as against each other and as against the relevant clearance system and the depository banks.

These questions, although fundamental, go far beyond the scope of the present chapter and can therefore only be touched on in so far as they impinge directly on the main object concerned, namely the perfection of a security interest of the bonds lodged in the relevant clearance system.

Euro-clear

The participants in the Euro-clear system, normally financial institutions, are bound by agreement to the published terms and conditions of Euro-clear which incorporate the operating procedures published by Morgan Guaranty, Brussels. The terms and conditions of Euro-clear are governed by the laws of Belgium. Each participant submits to the non-exclusive jurisdiction of the courts of Brussels for the purposes of any dispute. It is important to ensure therefore, on any security created is valid and enforceable under Belgian law. What would appear to be the dominant view of Belgian counsel which is accepted for the purposes of this discussion, is that the participant will be regarded as having a proprietary interest in securities held by Euro-clear in the securities clearance count of that participant. This view is not universally held and doubts have been expressed as to whether it is, indeed, correct. The issue is dependent on an interpretation of the terms and conditions of Euro-clear and the applicability of Belgian statute, the full details of which cannot be fully analysed here.

Assuming the view of Belgian counsel, Euro-clear (or a depository for Euro-clear) holds the bonds of a certain type and issue on a fungible basis and these are regarded as the co-property of all participants whose securities clearance accounts are credited with them. It will be seen as this is also the case in respect of one type of securities account operated for participants by Cedel.

It is not possible to contribute here to the wider issue of a participant against a clearance system (or a depository for a clearance system) on its failure to return the securities lodged, although this issue is clearly of importance in relation to the bank's security over the bonds. To date, there is no indication, of such a situation ever having arisen in practice. As such, the issue is at present theoretical although it cannot be totally disregarded on this account.

Turning to the bank's security, from the point of view of Belgian law, provided the bonds are credited to the bank's securities clearance account with Euro-clear, they are regarded as being possessed by the bank. As a result, a valid pledge exists under Belgian law, not only between the bank and the counterparty but also *vis-à-vis* third parties including Euro-clear.

For a valid pledge to be created under Belgian law there must also be included in the synthetic securities contract sufficient identification of the bond pledge (type, issuer, principal and maturity) and of the obligation of the counterparty against which the pledge is made.

If the views taken by the participant of the bond clearance system has merely a contractual right against Euro-clear then the participant bank will hold the contractual right on trust for the counterparty. Accordingly the counterparty will have an equitable interest in the contractual right. In order to obtain security over the counterparty's interest the participant bank will need to take a charge over that equitable interest. It is impossible for the equitable interest to be signed by way of a legal assignment and accordingly the counterparty cannot give to any third party a better title than that given to the participant bank by way of charge. The participant bank, therefore, will rank in priority to any subsequent third party charge.

Cash collateral arrangements in terms of Belgian law are subject to the law of the jurisdiction in which the relevant cash count is kept. Since the cash account of the counterparty with the bank will not normally be maintained in Belgium, the bank's security in this connection will not be affected by Belgian law (except that, first in the case of a counterparty incorporated in Belgium, Belgian bankruptcy law may override the cash collateral arrangements as described, regardless of the country in which the account is maintained and secondly it is likely that each counterparty will ultimately be subject to the bankruptcy laws of the jurisdiction in which it is incorporated).

Cedel

Cedel (Centrale de Livraison de Valeurs Mobilières) is a limited company incorporated in Luxembourg. The legal relationship between Cedel and each participant is governed by the laws of the Grand Duchy of Luxembourg pursuant to Article 55 of the Cedel management regulations.

Securities can be held on either a fungible or non-fungible basis. If they are held on the latter basis, the participant remains the sole owner. If on the former, a 1971 Grand-Ducal Decree provides that participants depositing instruments of a particular class will own such instruments in common.

Apart from the depositor's ability to choose between a fungible and a non-fungible account, there are no significant differences between Cedel and Euro-clear.

Standard Conditions

Many of the terms and conditions to be included in the master sythentic securities agreement are regularly found in the standard instruments in the swap market. Since these are well documented, there is no need for them to be recited here. Certain of these do, however, need to be developed to take account of particular features of the sythentic security and some new conditions must be incorporated. These are now outlined briefly.

Payments

Generally, in the case of payments under swap agreements, it is the concern of each party to ensure that it does not make any payment without having received the payment corresponding to that payment.

In a synthetic security, there are no payments scheduled to be made by the counterparty but instead payments made by the bank are expressed to be conditional upon payment of the coupons under the bond. In practice, this procedure results in the bank being exposed in respect of mis-matched payments and therefore conditions must be incorporated to protect the bank's interest in such situations.

Thus, for example, if a fixed rate bond is involved, the coupon will be payable on a fixed date, normally on an annual basis. Where the synthetic interest is calculated on a floating rate basis, it will normally be payable in respect of three or six month periods. As a result, the bank will be exposed to the credit risk of the issuer of the bond, whom failing the counterparty, for a period which could extend to some months, depending on the relation between the coupon payment date and the dates fixed for payment of the floating rate note.

Provisions must therefore be incorporated in the master agreement allowing the bank to claw back any payments made by it on the occasion of its failing to receive the corresponding payment. In addition, interest should be provided for on the refunded payments at a rate representing the cost to the bank of funding such payments for the particular period. This is important, because it is likely that the bank will have covered its position in respect of the floating rate by using the fixed coupon under the bond to service a swap. If this income is not forthcoming then the bank will need to obtain funds from another source to fund the swap.

Causes of termination

The circumstances which give rise to an option to terminate on a no fault basis in standard swap agreements commonly comprise illegality, imposition of taxes and, more rarely, increased costs. In the case of synthetic securities, there must be added to this list the possibility of early redemption of, or default under, the bond or its coupons. The contract will often provide an option to terminate available only to the bank if such circumstances arise.

Loss on termination

Where, as a result of default of one of the parties in terms of the master agreement, the other party is entitled to terminate, the defaulting party will be liable to indemnify the other for the other's losses on termination.

Where termination is on a no-fault basis, an affected party is identified, who will be the counterparty in respect of default under the bond and otherwise the party or parties subjected to increased costs, the imposition of taxes or illegality. Only the affected party will be entitled to terminate the master agreement except in the case of default under the bond, when customarily only the bank may terminate.

The affected party will be required to indemnify the other for its losses or, if the other has made profits, the affected party shall be indemnified for its losses but only to the extent of the other's profits.

Such provisions are standard in swap agreements. As in other swap agreements, the main problems ensue from the attempt to quantify loss.

In a synthetic securities contract, the counterparty is under no obligation to make any periodic payments. The principal cause of default by the counterparty will therefore be in respect of its bankruptcy. The master agreement will provide for the bank to be indemnified for its losses as a result of the default by the counterparty. It is possible that the bank will not make any losses in these circumstances, because it will not have lost any source of income. It will, however, have little prospect of recovering from the counterparty if there is a subsequent default under the bond, and will as a consequence no doubt wish to unwind the synthetic security at that point, rather than carry this additional risk. In these circumstances, the charge should secure any losses on unwinding.

Similarly, where the counterparty is an affected party as described above, it is possible that the bank will make profits on termination, although in this case the bank will require to account to the counterparty for these profits to the extent of the counterparty's losses.

If, on the other hand, the bank defaults, the counterparty's losses will be the sum required to generate the remaining payments due by the bank in terms of the contract.

In relation to a synthetic securities contract, the bank will invariably seek to cover its position in respect of its payment obligations under the security by using the income stream available to it from the bond coupon. It is essential that the counterparty in the synthetic security is put on notice of this fact in the agreement so as to ensure that the bank will be entitled to claim from the counterparty on termination of the sythentic securities contract, all losses arising in respect of the cost to the bank of fulfilling the obligations it may have under any underlying agreement.[10]

Such a claim will arise on a no-fault termination. It will be most acute on the occasion of a default under the bond, principal or coupon, but also where the bank is an affected party as described above. The bank will of course be subject to the common law obligation to minimise its losses. One of the practical results of this will be that the bank may be required to take the least costly of the two options open to it in respect of any underlying arrangement, namely the unwinding of that arrangement or the purchase of an alternative income stream with which to service such an arrangement.

UK tax considerations

The Inland Revenue in the past analysed swap payments not as interest but as annual payments falling under s.349(1) of the Income and Corporation Taxes Act 1988 (the "Act"). As such, a concession was granted which, subject to certain conditions, exempted counterparties from the withholding tax obligation imposed by that section. Recently, however, the Inland Revenue have indicated that they do not now consider payments under a currency or interest rate swap to be annual payments. As such, there will be no obligation to withhold under that section. The Inland Revenue have not stated their present analysis of swap payments, but presumably they remain of the view that these are not to be regarded as interest and therefore within the ambit of the withholding obligations of section 349(2) of the Act.

This change in position of the Inland Revenue, while removing concerns about the withholding tax obligation imposed by section 349(1) raised the question of how certain counterparties could obtain a deduction against tax in respect of payments made under swaps.

The Inland Revenue addressed this question by stating that they are prepared to allow swap payments to be "treated" as annual payments in order that the payer might be able to deduct these as charges on its income under section 338(3) of the Act. This concession is subject to the proviso that the payments are either made under deduction of tax or the recipient is a recognised bank which received the payments in the ordinary course of its banking business.

Accordingly, the present analysis of the Inland Revenue whereby swap payments are not regarded as annual payments but may be deemed to be such under certain conditions thereby allowing the payer to obtain the benefit of a deduction under section 338(3) of the Act results in the same practical consequences as their former analysis whereby swap payments were regarded as annual payments but had the benefit of a concession.

The Inland Revenue have indicated that they view Asset Swaps, Collateralised Asset Swaps and Synthetic Securities in exactly the same way as typical liability swaps. The only direct tax problem relates to the amount of loss which can be claimed in respect of any purchase and sale of the security since, in computing the loss, the Inland Revenue consider that the present value of receipts under the transaction as a whole should be taken into account.

In relation to Collateralised Asset Swaps, however, there is an ancillary issue which has tax implications. Since the Bank has a charge over the bonds, these are held by the Bank on behalf of the counterparty. The Bank collects the coupon payments and applies these in satisfaction of the counterparty's obligations under the swap.

As such, the Bank is acting as coupon collection agent and is therefore subject to section 123 of the Act if the coupon is a "foreign dividend" as defined in that section. The most important implication of this is that an obligation to withhold tax in respect of the coupon payments will be imposed on the Bank unless it is proved that the party entitled to the coupons is not resident in the United Kingdom for the purposes of that section.

Consequently, it may prove that collateralised asset swaps with U.K. counterparties are not commercially viable due to this withholding obligation.

Regulatory concerns

The Basle Committee on Banking Regulations and Supervisory Practices comprising representatives of the central banks and supervisory authorities of the Group of Ten countries and Luxembourg produced in July 1988 its report on International Convergence of Capital Measurement and Capital Standards.

It is envisaged that the proposals contained in this report will be fully implemented by 1992 and the main significance of the report for the present purposes is the incorporation of off-balance-sheet activity of banks, including swaps and related instruments, within the capital adequacy framework.

The framework involves identifying each instrument's credit equivalent amount. The committee was not unanimous in agreeing the method of calculating this amount in relation to swaps and, as a result, two methods have been authorised. The first of these, named the "original exposure method" involves the application of a set of credit conversion factors to the notional principal amount of the instrument which vary according to its nature and maturity. The second, approved by the majority and designed the "current exposure method" involves the calculation of the sum of each instrument's current exposure and potential exposure (terms which will be discussed further below).

In each case the resulting amount is then assigned one of five risk weights according to the nature of the counterparty, the maturity of the obligation and any qualifying collateral or guarantees, in the same way as on balance sheet credit exposures.

There has, as yet, been no direct consideration by the regulatory authorities of the nature of synthetic securities. Accordingly, any comments on possible treatment of synthetic securities from a regulatory point of view can only be tentative at this stage.

Current exposure is equated with mark-to-market value on the reporting date. This is calculated on the basis of the amount the bank would have to pay to replace the net payment stream in the contract if the counterparty were to default. In a synthetic security, default of a counterparty would not, in the first instance, deprive the bank of any payment stream and as has been noted, it is probable that the bank will not suffer losses as a result of the counterparty's default. If the regulatory bodies make a similar analysis it is likely that a synthetic security would consistently have a lesser current exposure value for these purposes than a corresponding asset swap or collateralised asset swap.

Potential exposure is intended to account for the additional exposure which may arise over the remaining life of a contract as a result of fluctuations in interest rates. It is calculated by multiplying the notional principal amount of the contract by an applicable conversion factor.

Potential exposure, as defined, is common to all instruments in the swap market including synthetic securities and it is to be anticipated, therefore, that there will probably be no significant differences in the treatment of synthetic securities over other swap instruments in the calculation of potential exposure.

The collateral involved in synthetic securities transactions, as indeed in collateralised asset swaps, will be of limited benefit in reducing the risk for capital adequacy purposes. The existence of collateral is not recognised in calculating credit equivalent amounts. Further, in terms of the report, only collateral which comprises basically domestic national government debt will affect the assignment of risk weights.

International issues

To operate a synthetic securities programme effectively it will be necessary to be aware of the law of incorporation of the counterparty. In particular, it is essential to ensure that the bank's security will be effective against the counterparty on its liquidation under its jurisdiction of incorporation.

In addition, it will be important to ensure that there are no adverse tax implications of marketing the product and that marketing complies with the regulatory framework of each particular country. Thus, for example, it would appear that the Japanese Ministry of Finance will not regard a bond stripped of its coupons by anyone other than the issuer as a security for the purposes of their securities legislation. As such, anyone who wishes to deal in a synthetic security will require the consent of the Japanese Ministry of Finance.

Particular problems have been encountered in the past in connection with the sale of securities in the US and it is worth providing a little more detail on the possible problems which might be posed in selling synthetic securities within the US, or to US persons.

USA

It is well known that the term *security* is widely defined for the purposes of the US federal securities laws. Whether synthetic securities and for that matter, interest rate and currency swaps are to be regarded as securities for these purposes currently remains uncertain. There has been no pronouncement by the United States Securities and Exchange Commission (the SEC) which specifically addresses the status of such products in terms of this legislation.

On balance, it would appear, however, that the standard types of swap products are not generally regarded as securities for the purposes of the US federal securities' laws.[11] This view arises from an analysis of the customary features of swap agreements, and is based principally on the bilateral and conditional nature of the payment obligations and the standard prohibitions or stringent restrictions on transferability.

The differences to be detected between a synthetic security and other swap instruments render the status of the sythentic security more doubtful for the purposes of the US federal securities' laws. The possible analysis of a synthetic security as payment of a floating rate of interest by a bank (albeit dependent on receipt of a fixed rate coupon from a bond) in exchange for a price (albeit the consideration for the purchase of a bond) could easily lead to the synthetic security being classed as a security for the purposes of this legislation.

In order to avoid being subject to the US federal securities' legislation, it is likely that banks will restrict their market for synthetic securities in the first instance to sales outside the US to non-US persons, although they may, of course, take advantage of the well known private placement exemption under the US Securities Act 1933 which should allow the market to be extended to sophisticated institutional investors outside of the US, principally foreign branches of US banks.

Pending specific guidelines from the SEC, it is to be recommended that the standard selling restrictions developed in connection with Euro-commercial paper programmes be adopted for synthetic securities programmes to ensure that the bank as *issuer*, cannot be held liable for any contravention of the securities laws. In addition, the definition of US person should be extended to ensure that the synthetic security does not fall under the provisions of the US Tax Equity and Fiscal Responsibility Act.

This procedure is not ideal, not least because of the fact that the SEC have not approved such selling restrictions as the only US securities' law precautions for the initial offering of long-term securities into which category synthetic securities (if, indeed, they are securities) clearly fall. Obviously, however, the concept of a 90-day lock-up period which was developed in reliance on SEC staff no-action letters for long-term securities is hardly applicable to a synthetic security which is basically a bilateral contract.

The practical problem which is not resolved by the recommended practice relates to marketability. It is not clear when, if ever, a synthetic security subject to standard ECP selling restrictions will be regarded as *seasoned* for the purposes of the US federal securities' laws and thus free of any restrictions on re-sale. Marketability which is unrestricted by the provisions of the 1933 Act, will only be secured when the views of the SEC are made clear on what procedures would be acceptable for the seasoning of synthetic securities.

The status of the bond which is sold by means of a synthetic security must also be borne in mind for the purposes of the US federal securities' laws. Where such a bond has not been subject to the 90-day lock-up procedure, the legality of a sale to the foreign branch of a US person would depend on a number of factors, for example, the identity of the issuer and the marketability of the bonds in the US. These factors would need to be considered on a case-by-case basis and consequently the safest procedure is to require all bonds which are sold as part of a synthetic security to have been subject to the 90-day-lock-up procedure in connection with the initial offering. In addition, no circumstances should have come to the attention of the bank which might suggest that the distribution of the bond had not been completed.

Alternative structures

The charge over the bonds in a synthetic security may be popular with banks; however, it can pose serious problems for counterparties, particularly, as has been discussed, in relation to negative pledges. The counterparty must make a careful assessment of its position on entering a synthetic securities programme. If it discovers negative pledges by which it is bound and which would be breached by the terms of the synthetic security agreement, the only sensible course would be to seek the approval of the beneficiary of that negative pledge. Counterparties would be unwilling to do this, not least for reasons of business confidentiality.

Even if the current negative pledges given by the counterparty reveal no difficulty, it will be necessary for the counterparty to review the position on an ongoing basis to make sure that it does not subsequently enter into negative pledges which are automatically and immediately breached by the very existence of a charge under the synthetic securities agreement.

All of these concerns have led some banks to consider whether alternatives to a conventional synthetic security structure might exist which would avoid the need for the counterparty to create a charge over the principal of the bond. This is a process which is in its early stages. So far, attention has focused on the use of a technique well known in the asset sales market — sub-participation. Also, the interposing of a special purpose vehicle has been seen as a possible solution to some of the problems of developing instruments for re-packaging securities. We consider each option in turn.

Sub-participation

Essentially, this would involve the bank sub-participating a proportion of the relevant bonds to the counterparty on an interest rate basis which differs from that applicable to the bonds themselves. The bank would enter into an agreement with the counterparty in which the counterparty would pay to the bank, on commencement, the purchase price of the bonds, or a proportion thereof. In return, the bank would agree to pay to the counterparty an agreed interest stream calculated on an agreed basis (not that of the bonds) on the dates of the receipt by the bank of coupon payments in respect of the bonds.

The bank would retain legal ownership of the principal and coupons of the bonds and would lodge these in its own account with one of the clearing systems. As principal repayments were made with respect to the bonds, the bank would pay to the counterparty an amount equal to the counterparties' participation therein.

This sub-participation technique operates as an entirely *back to back* contract in which the financial risks associated with ownership of the bonds and coupons are transferred to the counterparty, but without any transfer of legal or beneficial ownership. A conventional sub participation (where the sub-participant's interest rate basis is the same as the selling bank's) normally results, it is understood, in off-balance sheet treatment for the relevant bonds and coupons for the selling bank, although this matter is presently under review by the regulatory authorities. Care must be taken to ensure that the change in interest rate basis does not affect the view of accountants and regulatory bodies in these respects.

Since the counterparty does not acquire beneficial ownership of the bonds this means that the bank's *swap risk* can be covered by means of a simple provision in the participation agreement under which the bank would be entitled, in the event that swap risk materialised, to sell the bonds and to apply the proceeds in satisfaction of any exposure on the counterparty. Whilst this achieves the commercial equivalent of a charge over the bonds, legally no charge is created and so one would not expect conventional negative pledges to be breached.

It should be noted, however, that the use of a sub-participation involves the counterparty in a double-credit risk for both principal and interest. This arises because, even if the issuer of the bond performs, if the bank defaults, the counterparty loses. In the asset sales market, this aspect has not yet caused difficulties and it should not therefore be expected to cause widespread difficulties in the synthetic security market (although this might change given Bank of England proposals for an additional weighting for capital adequacy purposes to reflect the double credit risk). Nevertheless, sub-participation may, initially, be a technique available only to the strongest of the banks selling such securities because counterparties, not used to sub-participation in this market, may be concerned by the additional risk element.

Special purpose vehicles

The utilisation of special purpose vehicles has been regarded by some as a panacea for all banking ills. While there is undoubtedly a place for such vehicles in the development of synthetic securities, they are by no means to be regarded as an appropriate course of action in all circumstances.

One undeniable advantage which a special purpose vehicle can offer, however, is freedom from adverse tax consequences. Thus, for example, a vehicle incorporated and resident in the Cayman Islands will normally be provided by the Cayman government with an undertaking that the vehicle will, in effect, be tax exempt for a period of 20 years from the date of such an undertaking.

Another advantage is the possible removal from the bank's books of securities which are held at a discount to par due to market conditions pertaining at the time, which the bank would gladly dispose of, but does not wish to sell, in the hope that market conditions might improve.

To effect this, the bank may sell the securities to a special purpose vehicle, who would finance the purchase by selling a re-packaged version of such securities. Thus, for example, the vehicle might re-package longer-term securities into short-term instruments, by financing the acquisition of the longer-term securities through an issue of commercial paper. The commercial paper would be of a maturity commensurate with the length of the interest period on the longer-term securities. The coupon on the longer-term securities would be used to fund the interest/discount element of the commercial paper and (subject to market conditions) the subscription monies of a subsequent tranche of commercial paper issued on the maturity date of the previous tranche would fund the repayment of principal of the maturing tranche.

The first problem which needs to be overcome in such a procedure concerns the fact that the bank and the vehicle must be completely independent. The bank or any of its subsidiaries must have no legal or beneficial interest in the vehicle's shareholding if they are successfully to dispose of such longer-term securities. The conventional method of engineering such a situation is for the vehicle's shares to be owned by a trustee company who would hold the shares on trust for general charitable purposes. The costs of such arrangements, together, of course, with the start-up and on-going costs of the vehicle need to be borne in mind in evaluating such a programme.

The second problem relates to the credit rating of the vehicle. If the vehicle has only a nominal share capital then it will clearly not be an attractive risk to investors. On the other hand, it is unlikely that the whole procedure would be viable on any other basis.

In operating a system of rolling over successive tranches of short-term securities, a problem arises concerning the possibility of the longer-term securities being redeemed mid-interest period, which could result in the redemption monies being insufficient to generate the amounts due in respect of the commercial paper maturing thereafter. This, and the risk that due to problems in the market, difficulties are occasioned in the sale of a tranche of commercial paper resulting in failure to redeem the maturing tranche, means that it is likely that the issues of commercial paper will need to be guaranteed in some way if they are to be readily marketable.

One method of providing some security for holders of the short-term securities would be for the vehicle company to secure each issue by executing a charge over the longer-term securities in favour of the holders of the commercial paper. If, however, these securities are held at a discount at par, such security may not be sufficient.

If the issuer of the longer-term securities is perceived to be a reasonable credit risk, (ie it is only the current illiquidity of the market which has caused such securities to be incapable of sale without incurring a loss) then the appropriate approach may be for the bank to grant a letter of credit in respect of the capital and not the interest element of the commercial paper. Otherwise, the letter of credit would need to guarantee both capital and interest.

There are numerous ancillary problems which need to be resolved in considering such a programme which have implications for the two major issues, namely, the cost of the programme and credit-rating: whether or not the vehicle should publish accounts; how the bank may extract profits; whether each vehicle should be restricted to one purpose, and whether the commercial paper should be lodged in a fungible or non-fungible account with a clearance system, in the name of the bank, the vehicle or the trustee of the holders of the commercial paper. Given that these issues relate, to a greater or lesser extent, to the use of special purpose vehicles in general rather than their use in the creation of synthetic securities, they will not be developed further in this chapter.

To sum up, the issues involved in setting up a synthetic securities programme by means of a special purpose vehicle are varied and complex. The cost implications probably mean that such a venture will only be embarked upon as a last resort. Nevertheless, special purpose vehicles do offer possibilities which other methods cannot offer and as such, their use, while limited, will continue to be significant.

[1] *Leitch & Co. v. Leydon* [1931] A.C. 90
[2] *Rolled Steel Products v. British Steel Corporation* [1985] 2WLR 908
[3] Section 5.2.2 Vol. 1 Gore-Browne on Companies, Jordan & Sons Ltd.
[4] *D.C. Thomson & Co. v. Deakin* [1952] Ch.646
[5] *In re Charge Card Services Ltd* [1986] 3 All E.R.289
[6] Tony Shea: Legal Analysis: Journal of International Banking Law, 1986 Vol. 1 Issue pp 192-198
[7] [1986] All E.R.673 see Tony Shea: Legal Analysis op.cit.pp 198-201
[8] Bankruptcy Act 1914 s.31 and Insolvency Act 1986 s.323
[9] *British Eagle International Airlines Ltd. v. Compagnie Nationale Air France* [1975] All E.R. 390
[10] For a full discussion of these issues see Schuyler K. Henderson, Exposure of Swaps and Termination Provisions of Swap Agreements, Cap.2, Part viii, Swap Finance vol. 2 ed. Boris Antl, Euromoney Publications, 1986.
[11] For a short introduction to this issue, Linda B. Klein, Interest Rate and Currency Swaps: Are they Securities? International Finance Law Review, October 1986, pp 35-39.

CHAPTER 10
Accounting and tax implications
by Emma Lubbock and Richard Kilsby

Introduction

This chapter is designed to illustrate the accounting implications of synthetic instruments and to explore the United Kingdom tax aspects of such transactions. Reference will also be made to alternative tax treatments which might apply in various overseas locations.

The first part of the chapter explores the background to current developments in accounting and how they might apply to such complex structures as synthetics. In order to be able to develop a clear set of guidelines to account for these transactions, it is necessary to examine the components of the transaction. However, under the current framework there is a potential conflict between accounting for the substance of the transactions and compliance with certain of the accounting requirements.

Accounting objectives

In general, the purpose of accounting is to provide a record of the transactions and business conducted by an organisation. However, this can be done with two completely different objectives in mind:

— economic performance measurement; or
— a measure of stewardship and prudence.

Traditionally, external financial reporting has been coloured by a significant element of the latter.

There are two main types of accounting:

Financial accounting	Management accounting
- Reporting to the 'outside world'	- Internal reporting
- Governed by rules (eg Accounting Standards)	- May be prepared in the manner most meaningful for their use
- No opportunity to supplement information or correct misunderstandings	- Further explanations/information can be provided as required
- Varied range of uses and users	- Defined range of uses and users

Ideally, the priniciples and policies followed should be the same in both types of accounting. However, because of the stewardship element of financial accounting, and in particular the need to achieve a degree of comparability and certainty in external reporting, a framework of rules needs to be developed.

Guidance on synthetics

Because synthetic instruments are a relatively new product, existing accounting rules do not specifically address this area. Synthetic instruments can cause problems from the accounting standpoint as they mix various existing products to produce a new product. Whilst in some countries (eg the US) a limited amount of guidance does exist on some of the individual instruments which go to make up a synthetic, the strict application of such rules may not always produce the correct result.

In the UK (and increasingly in other countries) it is generally accepted that the accounting should reflect the substance of a transaction rather than the legal form, although this position is not quite so clear cut as it might have been following recent developments concerning off-balance sheet finance schemes. In other words, accounting should aim to reflect the economic reality of the transaction. In particular, rewards need to be matched with the costs/risks which generate those rewards. This rule is particularly important, as the results obtained through accounting for individual elements of the synthetic separately can be quite different from those obtained by regarding the transaction as a single entity.

Basic products

The term synthetic can be used to describe a whole range of transactions (eg a synthetic future created by buying and selling options). However, for the purposes of this chapter, we will concentrate on the basic synthetic security (ie combining a bond with a swap). In particular, we will consider the following structures illustrated in Chapter 5.

Asset swap Under this type of swap, the investor buys the bond and acts as counterparty to the swap. The purchase of the bond and the swap may be undertaken simultaneously or may be undertaken at different times.

The Synthetic Security As a Synthetic Security, a new instrument is structured so that the investor buys only those components of the underlying instruments which contribute to the desired performance or behaviour, without any unwanted elements which are usually retained by the arranging bank.

A variation of the Synthetic Security where the bank itself buys the fixed rate bond and issues its own piece of paper against this bond. Again, from the investor's viewpoint there is a single security which can be traded. In some cases the paper issued by the bank specifically carries the credit of the bond issuer rather than the credit of the bank. In other cases the credit on the paper issued by the bank is the bank's own credit, or a combination of issuer and back credit.

Special purpose vehicle issue A special purpose vehicle issue of Synthetic Securities is one in which the arranger establishes a special purpose vehicle (SPV) which holds asset swaps created in the same manner as in the Synthetic Security structure and which issues new securities backed by these asset swaps. A variation of this is where the separate company buys a portfolio of bonds and then issues its paper against this, thus effectively creating a composite Synthetic Security. The packaging can also be applied to create a fixed coupon bond from an FRN.

The main accounting issues relating to synthetics include the following:
— How to recognise profit generated as a result of the synthetic instrument;
— Whether or not the synthetic instrument remains on the balance sheet of either the creator or the investor.

Accounting methods

Basically, there are two methods of accounting for synthetic transactions:
— the accruals methods; and
— the market value or the DCF method

We shall look first at the accruals method as this is perhaps the most common way of accounting for synthetics currently used. We shall then move on to look at the DCF method and discuss whether it provides a better way of accounting for this type of instrument.

Accruals method for asset swap

From the investor's perspective, the accounting method depends upon whether the synthetic is held for investment purposes or for trading purposes. Given the cumbersome structure of this type of transaction and the inherent lack of liquidity, it is likely that an investor undertaking such as asset swap will have the intention of holding the asset swap until maturity.

Accordingly, the bond would normally be held at cost with any difference between the cost and the maturity value amortised to profit over the life of the bond. The swap would then be accounted for on a normal accruals basis.

If the synthetic is held with the intention of reselling it, then it will be necessary to market value this security. This can be done by separately market valuing the bond and the swap. However, the cumbersome nature of this type of transaction for the purposes of creating a synthetic trading security is also reflected in the accounting treatment as market valuing a swap may be a difficult process for an investor.

From the perspective of the provider of the asset swap, it will merely have a swap with the investor as counterparty and this should be accounted for like any other swap which the bank may hold. Any profit made on the sale of the bond will be recognised at the time of sale except where the swap is done at non-market rates. In this case the profit recognised on sale of the bonds is adjusted and spread to match any loss or profit resulting from the non-market swap rate. This is similar to the treatment detailed below for a Synthetic Security.

Accruals method for Synthetic Security

Accounting from the point of view of the investor is relatively easy under this structure as the investor effectively owns an FRN. Thus, if the Synthetic Security is held for investment purposes, the bond will be held at cost (presumably par) and the floating rate interest recognised on an accruals basis.

If, however, the Synthetic Security is held for trading purposes it can be market valued like any other FRN using some sort of redemption yield calculation and the resulting profit or loss recognised immediately.

Accounting from the point of view of the provider is more interesting. The bank may well have purchased the fixed rate bond at a significant discount. It will then strip the coupons from the bond and sell the bond on to the investor at par with a floating rate coupon attached to it. Prima facie therefore the investment bank will have made a profit equal to the discount on the fixed rate bond. This profit will consist of two elements:

— part of the profit will compensate the bank for the difference between the fixed rate received on the stripped bond coupons and the fixed rate paid out under the swap agreement. Presumably one of the reasons that the bond is trading at a discount is that the coupon on the bond is lower than current market rates. Thus, it may well be the case that in order to achieve a floating rate receipt on the swap which is equal to the floating rate paid to the investor, the bank will have to pay a fixed rate which is above the fixed rate received on the stripped bond coupons.
— part of the profit on the sale of the bond will be pure arbitrage profit. For example, the bond purchased may be a 'dog bond' and thus the discount may be greater than that warranted purely by the interest rate differentials. This part of the profit represents pure arbitrage profit obtained by the investment bank for its repackaging service.

Under an accruals method of accounting the part of the profit relating to interest rate differentials should clearly be deferred and spread over the life of the swap to compensate for the loss on the swap transaction.

Under a strict accruals method the pure arbitrage profit would also be deferred and spread over the life of the transactions. However, there is an argument for taking the pure arbitrage profit upfront and merely deferring the interest rate differential. However, this is not quite the whole story. The so-called arbitrage profit is not only compensating the bank for its repackaging ability but is also compensating the bank for the credit risk which it has on the transaction. This credit risk comes from two sources:

— there is a credit risk to the bond issuer that for some reason the issuer will cease to pay the fixed rate coupon on the bond;
— there is also a credit risk to the swap counterparty as there is in any other type of swap.

There is an argument for deferring part of the arbitrage profit to compensate the bank for the credit risk that it is undertaking.

The above explanations deal with a Synthetic Security where a fixed rate bond is transformed into a synthetic FRN. However, similar concepts are applied where an FRN is turned into a synthetic fixed rate bond. The same types of arguments also apply to a structure where the bank retains the bond and issues its own paper against it. However, the amount deferred to compensate for the credit risk may need to be increased depending upon where the principal credit risk to the bond issuer lies.

Accruals method for special purpose vehicles

From a profit recognition standpoint, the accounting treatment for a synthetic transaction undertaken through a separate finance vehicle is similar to that for the Synthetic Security described above.

DCF or market value method

One alternative to the accruals method which has been canvassed is so-called market value accounting. A problem with this is that the conceptual framework in the US does not permit revaluation of liabilities and is largely based on historical cost accounting. Thus, assets held for trading purposes and available for resale will be accounted for on a market value basis; others will be held at historical cost. There are many inherent problems in applying market valuation techniques including the following:

Realisability The original justification for market valuing trading assets is that they are readily realisable in an active, deep and liquid market. It is therefore reasonable to regard marked to market profits as realisable even if not realised. This, of course, is only true if the market is available in which to sell assets or to extinguish liabilities. With structures such as the basic asset swap, a question must exist as to whether or not an active market exists in the synthetic security itself. It may be possible to find a market for each of the constituent parts. However, does this really provide a true value for the synthetic?

For example, if the synthetic is based on a 'dog bond', the value of the synthetic as a whole may well be greater than the sum of the values of the constituent parts (the bond and the swap).

What price? It is sometimes difficult to identify a specifically verifiable external price to use given this market. For example, if one were to try to base the market value of a synthetic on the market values of the constituent parts, it may be that, say, the market value quoted for the bond is not a true value due to the thinness of the market.

Credit and settlement risk The use of market valuation techniques automatically front ends profit on the transaction at a given point in time. It effectively ignores any continuing credit risk which may exist and any settlement risk arising in the future.

Recognition of profits and losses in cash There is a fundamental difference in marketing to market instruments where profits or losses are realised in cash or cash equivalent and one where there is no interim realisation of the marked to market profits or losses. For example, many synthetic security structures depend for their overall profitability on the reinvestment income on the cash surplus arising from the purchase of the bond at market value and the sale of the stripped bond at par. This reinvestment income will not tend to be recognised under a market valuation method.

In practice, the objective is not actually to arrive at a realisation or liquidation valuation but to measure the movement in intrinsic worth of the portfolio. For this reason, a better measure might well be a discounted cash flow basis, as follows:
— Identify all the cash flows inherent in all legs of the transaction;
— discount these cash flows in the currency in which they arise at an appropriate risk free rate, eg zero coupon rate or inherent yield redemption rate on US treasuries of appropriate maturity. This will involve constructing a yield curve and interpolating rates;
— translate the present values dervied into base currency at the spot rate;
— eliminate an element to be deferred in respect of credit risk and continuing administration/operational costs;
— recognise immediately the remaining present value of the profit or loss.

The main practical difficulty is to develop a framework to determine how much should be deferred in respect of credit risk. Many of the instruments traded do not inherently carry a full credit exposure.

Some institutions have developed matrices which enable them to develop the credit exposure in more detail for the newer trading instruments. Some factors which need to be taken into account include:
— volatility of the price which determines the market risk associated with closing out a position if a counterparty should fail;
— the period for which the transaction is outstanding;
— the timing of the cash flows, eg the payment and receipt of notional interest on the swaps (semi versus annual etc);
— whether notional or actual principal exchanges occur;
— the method of settlement.

Other practical problems with a DCF accounting method are:

What discount rate should be used? A number of alternatives suggest themselves — the reinvestment rate for cash surpluses; the borrowing rate for cash deficits; the hurdle rate of return imposed by the individual institution; some rate limited to the swap rate.

This is an area where more work still remains to be undertaken. However, whatever rate is finally selected it is important that it is consistently applied to all cash flows.

How should cash flows be grouped? It may be impractical to expect all daily cashflows to be discounted at separate rates throughout the portfolio. Accordingly, it may be necessary to group cash flows into 'time frames' which usually lengthen the further one moves away from the present. However, this can cause problems. Two cash flows which are perhaps a week apart in reality may appear six months apart if they happen to fall either side of the line dividing the time frames. This could have a significant effect on the overall DCF valuation. In practice, this can be overcome by testing the sensitivity calculation to slight shifts in the time frame pattern.

Accounting in the US

In the US the accruals method of accounting for synthetics is still very much the norm. However, the rules for deferring profits and losses on the front end sale of the bonds are perhaps stricter and better defined. This profit will be classified as a hedge profit provided that it can be demonstrated that the bond and the swap are linked and that there is close correlation between the bond and the terms of the swap.

Indeed, the US guidance goes further. It would appear that it is permissible for any premium on the synthetic transaction (ie what we referred to earlier as the 'arbitrage profit') to be recognised at the front end rather than being spread over the term of the transaction.

Whether US rules would allow DCF accounting is uncertain at present. Indeed current rules prevent US entities from revaluing liabilities.

Balance sheet treatment

Whether or not synthetic transactions are on-balance sheet or off-balance sheet for the provider depends on where the risk lies. In an asset swap the bank has only the swap transaction and therefore would include on the balance sheet the amounts which it would normally include for the same type of swap. Thus, the notional principle underlying the swap would not appear on the balance sheet whilst the accrued interest payable and receivable would appear on the balance sheet. These accruals would appear gross on either side of the balance sheet unless some legal right of offset existed between the payables and receivables.

For the Synthetic Security described above, the credit risk on the bond clearly lies with the investor and therefore the bank would be unlikely to show the bond on its balance sheet. The only amounts to appear on the investment bank's balance sheet would be the various interest accruals on the swap and on the fixed interest receivable from the bond issuer and the floating rate interest payable to the investor. Again, amounts may be netted only where there is a legal right of offset between payables and receivables.

Where the bank buys and holds the bond itself and issues paper against the bond, and where there is an explicit passing through of credit risk to the investor — where the investor's credit risk is directly to the bond issuer and not to the investment bank — then there is an argument for netting off the principal receivable on the bond with the principal payable to the holder of the synthetic instrument. However, before this can be done it must be certain that the investor has no recourse to the bank in the event of the issuer defaulting.

Where the transaction is undertaken through a separate financing vehicle, although the investor's credit risk is effectively to the bond issuer this is implicit rather than explicit. In other words, the strict legal position is that the investor's credit risk is to the financial vehicle which in turn has a credit risk to the bond issuer. Accordingly, in the accounts of the finance vehicle the bond should be shown on the balance sheet with corresponding liabilities to the investor on the other side.

There remains the question of whether or not the financial vehicles should then be included in the balance sheet of the investment bank itself. This is a vexed question and one about which there is currently much debate between the accounting and legal professions. The accounting profession would argue that where any risk remains with the investment bank, then the finance vehicle should be consolidated in the accounts of the investment bank, whether or not it is a subsidiary in the strict legal sense. The lawyers will no doubt argue the opposite case. Where the investment bank retains no risk on the transaction, current accounting practices would allow the whole deal to remain off-balance sheet. However, in order to avoid a moral obligation which may affect how the vehicle is viewed, finance vehicle must not use the name of the investment bank nor hold itself out to be of a similar credit standing to the investment bank. In other words, the investor must realise that the investment bank has merely packaged the synthetic security and is not substituting itself as the credit risk on it.

Where a transaction is constructed such that the investment bank sells the bond but guarantees performance on the bond in order to raise the bond's credit standing, it is at present uncertain whether or not this type of transaction would be on or off-balance sheet. Where the bond is sold to the investor the transaction would probably be off-balance sheet in line with other guarantees and would be shown as a contingent liability. However, if such a scheme were transacted with a separate finance vehicle then there is a strong argument that the finance vehicles should be consolidated thus bringing the transaction on-balance sheet. This is a complex area and one which has not been fully resolved by the accounting profession.

US formal guidance

Whilst there is no formal accounting guidance in the US which deals specifically with synthetics, it could be argued that the balance sheet treatment of such a transaction falls under the scope of FAS 77 — *Reporting by Transferors for Transfers of Receivables with Recourse.* This standard lays down three conditions which must be satisfied before such a transaction can be treated as a sale of receivables and hence for the receivable to be removed from the balance sheet. These conditions are:
— The transferor must surrender control of future economic benefit embodied in the receivables transferred;
— The transferor's obligation under any recourse provisions can be reasonably estimated;
— The transferee cannot require the transferor to repurchase the receivables except pursuant to the recourse provisions.

If any of the above conditions fail to be satisfied then the receivables must be left on the balance sheet with the funds received from the transferee shown as a liability.

In the asset swap structure, there is little doubt that the sale of the bond to the investor appears to satisfy the above three criteria and the bond can therefore be removed from the balance sheet. As in the UK, the investment bank is left only with an interest rate swap.

Under the Synthetic Security structure where the investment banks strips the fixed interest coupon from the bond before onselling the bond to the investor, there must be a question as to whether the first condition is satisfied. It could be argued that the bank has purchased two receivables —
— the right to receive periodic fixed interest payments;
— the right to receive principal repayment at maturity.

The investment bank has only transferred the second of those receivables but has retained control over the economic benefit of the interest flows. Hence, it could be argued that the purchase price of the bond should be split between principal and interest flows and that only those parts relating to the principal can be removed from the balance sheet. Likewise, the funds paid by the investor should be allocated between the amount relating to the bond and that relating to the floating rate interest — the latter of these amounts to be included as a liability as the balance sheet.

Where the bank issues its own paper directly secured on the bond, a doubt must exist as to whether any asset transfer has actually taken place and hence it is probable that both the bond and funding would be stated gross either side of the balance sheet.

In the case of the special purpose vehicle structure it is probable that the three conditions specified in FAS 77 have been satisfied and hence the asset can be removed from the balance sheet. However, under certain structures it is possible that the transaction may fail the economic control test and in such circumstances the balance sheet would need to be grossed up.

Retention of credit risk by the investment bank does not necessarily preclude the removal of an asset from the balance sheet. Accordingly, an investment bank which seeks to enhance the credit on a synthetic by adding its own guarantee does not automatically impair the off-balance sheet treatment of the synthetic, although such a guarantee would need to be shown as a contingency in the same way as other guarantees.

Summary

In general terms it is true to say that in the UK the accounting treatment for synthetics follows the substance of the transaction rather than the strict legal form. Many banks still employ the accruals method of accounting for such transaction which with current structures is probably just about manageable. However, as the concepts underlying synthetic securities become better understood and there is a consequent increase in the complexity of such arrangements, the application of accruals accounting may well become more and more difficult and more banks may well switch to a DCF method of accounting for this type of transaction. This, in turn, will lead to greater research on the credit risks inherent in such deals and a more defined method of identifying the reward necessary to compensate for this credit risk. This will allow a more accurate assessment of the arbitrage earned by the bank.

From the investor's perspective, the key is really substance over form. Investors should account for synthetic transactions in the same way in which they would have undertaken their accounting if they had brought the real security. For example, a synthetic FRN should be accounted for by the investor in the same way as a real FRN.

The question of whether these types of transaction are on or off-balance sheet for the investment bank depends on where the various credit risks lie. However, the debates about separate finance vehicles look set to continue for some time to come.

In the US the rules would appear to be a little stricter so that the way in which the transaction is structured may require more attention. As in the UK, the accruals method is still the most common way of accounting for synthetics although there would appear to be no reason why a DCF based method could not be adopted for such transactions. Whilst US accounting does not allow the revaluation of liabilities, the revaluation of both assets and swaps is permissible. Again, care may need to be taken in structuring the arrangement if this accounting methodology is adopted. The balance sheet treatment falls under FAS 77 and would appear to be more lenient than in the UK as the guaranteeing of the credit risk on the synthetic by the investment bank would not appear to impair the off-balance sheet status.

Elsewhere, the accounting rules may produce some unexpected results. For example, in many European countries securities are valued at the lower of cost and market value and unrealised profits cannot be recognised. In such an environment it may be necessary for the investor to recognise a loss on the bond at the front end if the bond is purchased at par from the investment bank. This is particularly a danger in the asset swap structure where the market value of the security is clearly visible. The future profit on the swap could not be recognised as it would be unrealised. In such circumstances, it may be necessary to restructure the deal to make it more acceptable to the investor.

Synthetic instruments are complex transactions and accounting needs to be carefully formulated. However, in an ideal world accounting should never be the major determinant of whether or not a transaction should be undertaken. If a transaction makes sense from a commercial standpoint then it should be worth doing; accounting should adapt itself to try and reflect this commercial reality.

Tax implications: introduction

The purpose of the second section of this chapter is to consider the UK tax issues raised by the creation of synthetics. Reference will also be made to tax treatment in the US, Australia and Japan.

The performance of many individuals and the departments in which they work is judged by reference to management accounts which are drawn up on a pre-tax basis. Nevertheless, for the company as a whole it is essential to measure the profitability of any transaction on a post-tax basis. This applies not only to companies investing in financial instruments but also to the arranging bank involved in packaging and marketing these instruments.

Our experience to date suggests that most companies are looking for certainty of tax treatment. Unfortunately, this can be very difficult to provide. In today's rapidly changing world, new financial instruments and techniques are being developed in the capital markets area all the time. The Inland Revenue's understanding of these techniques inevitably lags behind and new legislation to cope with new products takes time to be developed.

Key UK tax issues

The tax issues may be illustrated by using the US dollar FRN as the example of a typical synthetic. The questions which we need to ask ourselves are:

— Will all payments qualify for tax relief?
— Can all payments be made gross?
— How will any gains be taxed?
— When will payments/receipts be recognised for tax purposes?

These questions will be addressed first in relation to the investor and then to the arranging bank in respect of the asset swap and the Synthetic Security, including the special purpose vehicle issue.

Asset swap: investor's perspective

The tax treatment of the home-made asset swap is relatively straightforward from the investor's point of view. The investor owns a bond carrying a fixed rate coupon and he is party to a separate interest rate swap. In general, the two legs of the transaction will be looked at in isolation and the investor will not be regarded as having entered into a simple composite transaction.

Interest will be received on the bond and, assuming that this is a quoted Eurobond, will generally be received gross. In the case of a bank or financial trader, interest will be taxed as trading income based on the amount booked in the financial accounts. For other investors interest will be taxed when received under schedule D case III.

The tax treatment of swaps is fairly well understood (at present, although an Inland Revenue paper on the topic is expected soon). The key points to note relate to arrangement and swap fees and forward foreign exchange contracts.

Arrangement fees

The arrangement fee is not likely to be deductible for UK purposes if it is paid by an investment company. A trading company (including a bank) which enters into a swap transaction may be able to obtain a tax deduction for the expenditure if it is for trading purposes and connected with trading assets or short-term borrowing where the interest is deductible as a trading expense. However, particularly for a non-bank trading company, it is possible that the expenditure will not be allowable as being held to be capital expenditure.

Swap fees

The periodic swap payments calculated by reference to interest would generally be allowable in the UK on a paid basis (though a bank or certain other financial institutions may be able to apply an accruals basis).

The Inland Revenue have, in the past, viewed these amounts as annual payments for UK tax purposes. This means that income tax would normally be required to be deducted at source from the swap payments. By concession, the Inland Revenue have accepted that this is unnecessary where the payments are made to or by a recognised bank in the UK acting as *principal* (*not* agent) and the fees are calculated by reference to interest rate differentials. There are strong grounds for arguing that this is not technically correct but as it provides both freedom from withholding tax and tax relief for the expenditure in most cases (a possible exception being currency coupon payments) it has been generally welcomed as a pragmatic solution to the problem.

The Inland Revenue have extended the concession to payments of swap fees made by a financial trader other than a bank but payments to such a trader are still subject to withholding tax unless the payer is itself a bank or financial trader. The withholding tax exemption for transactions with recognised banks gives these companies an essential role as an intermediary for UK counterparties. Some care is required by non-bank counterparties to ensure, first, that the bank is recognised as a bank for the purposes of this exemption and second, that the bank is really acting as principal in the transaction.

Forward FX contracts

The most severe complication for a UK participant in a swap transaction arises in respect of the gains or losses arising on the foreign currency in a currency swap. In the case of an investment company the foreign currency is a chargeable asset for capital gains purposes. The same would also apply to most trading companies but not to a bank or other concern with a trade in which the gains from such foreign currency transactions fall to be dealt with as part of trading income.

Where a swap is used to hedge a capital liability, such as a long-term borrowing, a tax mismatch arises which can effectively destroy the hedge. For example, if there is a gain on the forward exchange agreement in the swap the resulting charge to capital gains tax will not be reduced by the corresponding loss on the long-term borrowing, since gains or losses on capital liabilities are outside the scope of capital gains tax. In the case of an asset swap the position may be less serious since any movement on the swap will normally be matched by a corresponding movement on another capital asset and the mismatch resulting from the asymmetrical treatment of capital assets and liabilities may not occur.

Asset swap: bank's perspective

When the Inland Revenue were approached on the tax treatment of synthetics in the summer of 1986, their view was that an asset swap should be fragmented and each leg of the transaction looked at at separately. This view was consistent with the prevailing trend by the Revenue to view hedging transactions in isolation rather than match hedges with specific underlying assets or transactions and tax them accordingly.

The effect of this treatment would be to recognise immediately the profit or loss earned by the arranging bank on the disposal of the Eurobond. The corresponding profit or loss on the swap agreement would, however, normally be deferred over the life of the swap, thus resulting in a mismatch.

Since 1986, however, the Inland Revenue have become concerned that, in the case of certain investment banks which specialise in particular types of asset swaps, this treatment leads to a distortion of the taxable profits. For example, some European banks have specialised in purchasing bonds at a premium and shortly afterwards selling them at a loss packaged with a matching, but profitable, interest rate swap. Under European accounting conventions the loss on the disposal of the bond is recognised immediately, while the profit on the interest rate swap is deferred over the life of the agreement. This application of the 'prudence accounting' concept results in a significant deferral of tax liability and it is this distortion to which the Inland Revenue are objecting.

The Inland Revenue have taken the position that the tax treatment for the arranging bank will be determined by posing the question 'Would the arranging bank, acting reasonably, have entered into one leg of the transaction without the other?'. If the answer to that question is 'No' the asset swap will be treated as a single composite arrangement with profits and losses being matched for tax purposes. Following this change in attitude it is likely that the Inland Revenue will be making much more detailed enquiries into these transactions in order to identify asset swaps where the bond and swap are sold at compensating off market rates. Since there may be further significant changes in the tax treatment of asset swaps, investors would be well advised to obtain up-to-date tax advice from their professional advisers.

Synthetic Security: investor's perspective

We have already seen that, from an accounting viewpoint, the investor is regarded as owning an FRN. For tax purposes the same treatment is likely to apply and the investor will be taxed on the floating rate interest on an accruals basis (for banks and financial traders) or on a received basis (for other corporates). There is a technical argument that the securities will fall within the accrued income scheme so that the investor would be taxed on a proportion of the fixed rate bond coupon beneficially owned by the arranging bank. In view of the Revenue's current acceptance that the investor is the owner of a floating rate note the risk of the Revenue applying the accrued income scheme is slight.

Any adjustments made in the financial accounts, for example in the case of banks and financial traders to mark the FRNs to-market at the year end, will generally be accepted for tax purposes provided that they are applied on a consistent and even-handed basis. The Inland Revenue are likely to resist any attempt to value FRNs at the lower of cost or net realisable value, thus recognising unrealised losses but not unrealised profits for tax purposes. This treatment has in the past been adopted by some of the European banks operating in the UK but is not widespread.

Synthetic Security: bank's perspective

The Inland Revenue's current attitude towards Synthetic Securities is that these instruments should be treated as a single composite arrangement or blended product. In general, the Revenue will be prepared to accept the accounting treatment, subject to the proviso that this does not result in a distortion of taxable profits. The effect of this is that:
— the part of the profit relating to interest rate differentials may be deferred over the life of the swap;
— the part of the profit which represents pure arbitrage profit may be spread but only if it can be demonstrated that the profit relates to a continuing credit risk which the bank has to bear over the life of the Synthetic.
Again, the Inland Revenue will need to be assured that the accounting treatment is reasonable and it is likely that they will ask searching questions about the treatment of Synthetics in order to satisfy themselves on this point. The queries may cover areas such as:

The method used to compute the profit on the transaction   How scientific is it? How is credit risk identified? Is profit which has been earned being deferred? Questions may in particular be expected to be addressed to branch banks which are not subject to UK audits and where the accounting treatment is determined by accounting standards and concepts which apply in the home country. Particular attention is likely to be paid to banks which are operating in a particular specialist area of the market, for example buying up bonds and realising an immediate loss on their disposal on repackaging.

The method used to recognise unrealised gains and losses   The Inland Revenue are concerned that mismatches can arise — particularly in the case of foreign currency translations — because of differences in accounting treatment.

Intragroup or intrabank transactions   It is common for the different legs of a synthetic transaction to be carried out in different departments of the same bank or even in different legal entities within a financial group. Again, the Inland Revenue will need to satisfy themselves that there is no serious distortion of the UK taxable profits resulting from mismatches in the accounting treatment between these different entities. Where two separate legal entities are concerned, the Inland Revenue may invoke transfer pricing legislation if they are not satisfied that the UK taxable entity is receiving a market rate of return on the services it performs. Where different branches of a single legal entity are concerned the position may be even more complex. Essentially, it will be necessary to demonstrate that the profits attributable to the UK branch adequately reflect the economic value of the work undertaken by it.

Special purpose vehicle issues

The tax treatment for both the investor and the investment bank where the repackaging involves a special purpose vehicle (SPV) is generally more straightforward. Repackaging is isolated into a single vehicle and the tax treatment will, subject to the comments made above, generally follow the accounting treatment. Thus, for example, as explained in Chapter 5, where the SPV makes a public issue in the Euromarkets lead managed by the arranging bank, the investor will hold Eurobonds on which interest will be paid gross, such interest being subject to tax under the normal rules for Eurobond interest.

The tax position of the SPV itself, must, however, be considered carefully. For example, it is likely to be critical that the SPV is able to receive interest on the underlying securities gross either under the terms of an appropriate tax treaty or under the domestic legislation applicable to the securities (eg UK tax legislation for UK gilts). The SPV is unlikely to qualify for the concessionary treatment afforded to banks and financial traders and may therefore be unable to receive or pay swap fees gross.

In addition, it will be important to ensure that the SPV pays little or no tax on the income it receives and that the set up and running costs are kept to a minimum. These objectives may frequently be met by using an offshore vehicle.

Although the tax treatment of special purpose vehicles used to issue synthetic FRNs is relatively straightforward, it should be remembered that such vehicles may be used to create a wide variety of asset backed securities. Special purpose vehicles may take the form of a bare trust, a unit trust or a company. It is not within the scope of this chapter to consider the UK tax implications of all the alternatives. However, in each case it is important to consider the interaction between the tax liability of the investors and the SPV and in particular to avoid the following pitfalls:

— distributions by the SPV being subject to withholding;
— investors being taxed on income of the SPV on an arising basis irrespective of whether that income is actually distributed or not;
— tax being charged on the SPV on disposal of its assets and again on the investors on disposal of their securities thus resulting effectively in a double layer of taxation;
— adverse VAT implications on disposal by the SPV of its assets;
— capital duties on formation of the SPV and stamp duty/stamp duty reserve tax or other transfer taxes on transfer of the assets.

Special purpose vehicles may be used by banks and other financial traders to take assets off balance sheet. In this case, it may also be necessary to consider whether the SPV is or should be within the corporate tax or VAT group. Since the tax ramifications can become extremely complex it is often worth posing the question — could the same commercial effect be achieved in a simpler, more tax efficient way? In some instances, sub-participations may provide an elegant solution.

US tax issues

In an asset swap where the investor is the owner of the fixed coupon bond and party to the swap, the two legs of the transaction will be dealt with separately and the investor and the arranging bank will be taxed accordingly.

If the arranging bank has purchased a bond at a premium and immediately sold it at par packaged with a profitable swap, the Internal Revenue Service (IRS) are likely to argue that the market value of the bond is best evidenced by the cash received (par) plus the fair value of the swap. Presumably this amount would approximately equal the amount paid for the bond and, as such, no loss would be recognised upon disposition. The swap would then have a tax basis equal to its fair value (or the amount of the bond premium). In taking this view the IRS are not treating the asset swap as an integrated or composite transaction but merely applying market value rules to determine the profit or loss earned. If the arranging bank has held the bond for a time before packaging it with a swap, it may have elected to amortize the premium over par over the life of the bond. In this case, the basis for determining the bank's gain or loss will be par plus the unamortized portion of the bond premium at the date of disposal.

Although there are broad similarities between the treatment of synthetics under US and UK tax law, there is very little specific guidance in the US. As such, the tax treatment is uncertain. From the investor's perspective, tax issues in the US which must be considered are:

— Whether the swap payments and receipts are trade or business deductions and income or interest? Are they taxable at time of payment or receipt or some other date? What is the character of the swap — ordinary or capital?

— Can arrangement fees or other upfront fees, such as assumption or assignment fees, be amortized over the life of the related swap or must the fees be included in taxable income when received.

The arranging bank must also consider the issues raised above, and whether the interest rate swaps are 'inventoriable securities' for which the 'mark-to-market' method of tax accounting, as opposed to the historical cost method, would be permitted. There is no clear answer to many of these questions in the US.

Where a special purpose vehicle is being used the investor will be regarded as the owner of the new securities and will be taxed on the income accordingly. As in the UK the most critical question will generally be to ensure that the SPV qualifies for pass through status. In the absence of pass through status, the US system of double taxation (ie corporate and shareholder level tax) would result in corporate tax at the SPV level with only net profits being available for distribution to investors.

Australian tax issues

Asset swap: investor's perspective

A straightforward asset swap is treated as two separate transactions for Australian tax purposes — a fixed interest bond and an interest rate swap. Interest income from the bond is assessed for tax in the normal way, although the timing of the assessment depends on the nature of the investor.

For a 'pure investor' (where the bond is not held as part of a business) the interest income is returned on a receipts basis. For financial institutions and other businesses the basis of returning interest for tax is not settled, the better technical view being that interest income should be returned when due and payable under the contract. Nevertheless, the Australian Tax Office argues that a full accounting basis should be adopted and many taxpayers do in fact adopt this treatment.

A trader in bonds may recognise any profit or loss (the market premium/discount) arising on a bond which is trading stock prior to maturity through a trading stock tax valuation, but otherwise such a profit or loss can only be recognised on actual disposal of the bond. For a pure investor such a profit or loss will be dealt with under the capital gains tax provisions. Under these rules a profit is indexed for inflation if the bonds are held for more than 12 months, whereas losses are not indexed and are only deductible against capital profits and not against ordinary income such as interest.

Periodic swap payments are assessable and deductible for tax purposes. The timing of recognition of swap payments for tax purposes is not settled but again the better technical view is to recognise the payments for tax purposes on the date they become due and payable under the swap contract.

Generally, there is no Australian withholding tax on swap payments to non-residents and there is no withholding of ordinary tax on the payment of interest of swap payments to residents.

No profit or loss arising on a swap prior to maturity due, for example, to a movement in market fixed interest rates will be recognised for tax, although if the swap is novated or otherwise disposed of at a profit or loss prior to maturity, such profit or loss will be assessable or deductible for tax. Again, for a pure investor such profit or loss will be dealt with under the capital gains tax provisions. Even if the investor is a dealer in securities, trading stock tax valuation, which would enable the dealer to recognise the profit or loss prior to maturity, is not permitted because, in the absence of a swap secondary market, it cannot be argued that swap contracts constitute trading stock.

If the contract is a currency swap the tax consequences will be the same as for an interest rate swap, except that the exchange gain or loss arising on the maturity of the swap will be assessable or deductible for tax. In practice, formal notice may have to be lodged with the Australian Taxation Office to claim a loss. Any unrealised exchange gain or loss arising prior to maturity cannot be recognised for tax.

Finally, it should be possible to structure the transaction so that most if not all of any fee paid by the investor for the asset swap arrangement is deductible for tax purposes.

Synthetic Security: investor's perspective

The investor will be taxed on interest income in the same manner as for an asset swap.

The tax treatment of profits or losses arising on disposal of the Synthetic will follow that for bonds but with one important exception. Since there is at present no secondary market for Synthetic Securities, the trading stock valuation concession will not be available.

Arranging bank's perspective

The arrangement is treated as three separate transactions for tax purposes — a fixed rate bond, a swap contract and a floating rate security/loan/deposit. In this respect, the Australian tax treatment of Synthetic Securities differs from that in the UK and US.

The tax treatment of the fixed coupon bond and the swap follows that for an asset swap and has been described above. Floating rate interest is deductible on a daily accounting accruals basis and Australian interest withholding tax is payable if the investor is non-resident. Any exchange gain or loss on the floating rate security/loan/deposit is assessable or deductible to ordinary income tax and the capital gains tax provisions are not relevant.

Special purpose vehicle: investor's perspective

The investor is regarded as holding a floating rate note and will be taxed on interest income as outlined above. The treatment of profits or losses arising on the FRN will, as explained above, depend on the nature of the investor and the degree to which the FRN is treated as having a secondary market.

The tax treatment of the special purpose vehicle mirrors that of the arranging bank in the case of a Synthetic Security. However, if the SPV issues the floating rate note offshore on a public or widely spread basis, a statutory exemption from Australian interest withholding tax may be available.

Japanese tax issues

Japanese tax law for corporations does not make a distinction between capital gains and ordinary income so that capital gains and losses of corporations are aggregated with all other items in computing taxable income. The principal tax issues related to synthetics are the timing of income and loss recognition and allocation of that income among related parties.

Banks use the accrual method for net swap payments. Net payments are generally not subject to the interest withholding tax rules as they are considered fees and not interest. Short-term assets and liabilities denominated in currency other than yen are translated at the year-end rate whereas long-term foreign currency denominated positions are generally valued at cost. Listed securities are valued at the lower of cost or market and future contracts (other than foreign currency) are valued at cost.

Corporations other than banks generally have more flexibility in recognising the income or loss from net swap payments and the cash method may be used in non-abusive situations. Most positions could be valued at cost.

SECTION 5

Summary and Conclusion

Section 5 provides a brief review of the major issues discussed throughout this book, speculates on the future market for synthetic instruments, and offers some tentative conclusions on the importance of this new market for issuers, investment bankers and, most importantly, for investors.

Section 5 comprises chapter 11, the concluding chapter of this book.

CHAPTER 11

The future for synthetic securities

Introduction

In this book we have discussed those factors which contributed to bringing about the market in synthetic securities; the methods used to price and the techniques used to create these instruments. We have also discussed some recent examples of synthetic securities and their effects on related markets.

In conclusion, and as a summary for those who have not read the entire text, it is worth spending a few moments reflecting on what has taken place so far and speculating on some of the likely trends for the future.

Development of the market

In the past few years the growth of the market in synthetic securities has been phenomenal. Six changes in the external environment have contributed to this growth. These are discussed in more detail in Chapter 1 and are reviewed here as part of our overall conclusions.

The market in *financial hedge technology*, in particular for interest rate swaps, has evolved from a boutique activity transacting on a matched counterparty basis to a full market with market makers running open positions in swaps. Currency swaps have also evolved considerably and are now available continuously in the major currencies. Long-term bond options, which are similar to options on swaps (swaptions), are in the process of extensive development. We expect broad application of options to synthetic securities in future. The improvement and commonality in valuation techniques across markets has resulted in much lower costs of executing these hedges, with a consequent increase in arbitrage volumes. (See Chapters 2 and 3 for a full discussion of the developments in bond and swap valuation techniques).

Banks have changed dramatically. Higher *capital ratios* have slowed bank asset growth and forced bankers to service their clients' needs for fund raising by turning to off-balance sheet techniques. These include making loans to major borrowers and then selling participations in the loans to other banks (a semi-securitised method of transferring assets) and buying bond issues to distribute in the professional market and to sell to investors (fully securitised).

The increase in capital ratios accelerated the move towards *securitisation*, which resulted in many commercial banks being disintermediated from the business of providing major borrowers with funding.

Some banks adjusted to the post-securitised environment quickly and set up in competition with the investment banks. These succeeded in servicing their traditional borrowers' financing needs by adapting to the use of the new securitised financial products. Others adjusted more slowly and soon found they did not have the products to maintain their business relationships with borrowers and were becoming *disintermediated from the process of raising capital*.

This *differential access to borrowers* fostered the trade in securitised and semi-securitised assets between banks with, and those without, access to borrowers.

However, the enthusiasm of lenders who reduced the size of their asset portfolios (in order to free up capital to support their new securities activities), quickly changed to disillusionment. The *quality of earnings* from the trading and distribution of securities proved to be both low and risky, while the fixed costs were high. As banks started focusing on their revenues, by reducing trading activities and rebuilding asset portfolios, they discovered that the types of asset available were predominantly securitised, and the returns were lower than had been available previously.

This combination of factors resulted in a major increase in the demand for high-yielding, money market based instruments which were substitutes for traditional syndicated loans, loan participations and direct lending to corporate borrowers.

Changes in the marketplace

The typical investor in the Eurobond market has changed over the past few years, and is now more likely to be a professional and bank fund manager rather than a private investor. This shift seems likely to continue as investment markets become more complex and interconnected. This trend will foster the development of synthetic securities as fund managers are better able to use financial engineering techniques.

Risk and reward

The amount of risk an investor takes in purchasing a security is a combination of credit, interest rate and liquidity risk (for a full discussion of investor risks see Chapters 1 and 5).

Yield and credit risk

The public debt markets frequently exclude issuers of certain types and credit quality from sectors of the market in which there is underlying investor demand. This may be because the size of the 'pocket' of investor demand may be either too small or too transient for a public issue to service effectively (Chapter 7 reviews this phenomenon for corporate borrowers in the public floating rate note market). In these cases, synthetic securities can offer a clear added value solution to the investor's need.

Yield and interest rate risk

Again, despite the enormous number and variation of type of issues in existence, the public markets are unable to cater for the the individual risk preferences of every investor. As investors become more familiar with the principles of synthetic securities and more experienced in using hedge techniques, there will be a proliferation of highly customised instruments to satisfy these individual requirements.

Yield and liquidity risk

There will always be a class of investors who will be willing to trade off liquidity against yield. This will allow derivative products, such a synthetic securities, to continue to play a role in the portfolio composition of such investors.

Advanced portfolio management techniques

Some of the principles used by synthetic securities can be considered advanced portfolio management techniques which have yet to be fully discovered by investors. These include changing the interest rate or currency basis of a portfolio without changing the credit composition. This is achieved by *not* divesting the underlying portfolio but by attaching a series of hedges to create asset swaps or synthetic securities with the desired currency and rate basis. Another technique is to apply interest rate swaps to a portfolio to artificially change the portfolio's duration or currency weighting without liquidating synthetic *short* positions in currencies in which there is no other way to be net short.

Customised portfolios

Many investors have requirements for specific assets which are not available in the secondary capital markets. At present, however, few investors have the capacity to originate these assets directly from issuers themselves. Investment banks with their combined ability to use the primary market to originate specific types of paper to satisfy pockets of investor demand (while the paper can be swapped to provide the issuer's desired liability currency and rate exposure) and their ability to take assets from the secondary market and, using the same swap techniques, create synthetic securities to exactly match investor's needs, can intermediate the asset selection process and provide value-added solutions for investors.

Changes in the bond market

In the primary market, many lead managers have bid issuers for new issues at spreads to risk-free securities which were clearly unprofitable, but which were justified in terms of building market share. This phase of the market's development is clearly temporary and, despite continued intense competitive pressure in the new issues market, predatory pricing in order to buy market share will decline in importance. This may result in better valued new issues and a more balanced approach to servicing the needs of issuers *and* investors. However, as the barriers to entry (apart from regulatory barriers) are not significant, new entrants can be expected to return whenever existing participants report strong earnings.

The secondary market will continue to *polarise* between those (few) liquid issues which have become industry benchmarks and which are actively traded by a number of market makers, and an increasing number of issues which are not liquid but which trade to value.

Innovation and liquidity

Many of the new types of paper and some of the financial instruments, launched onto the market in recent years have been fashionable only for as long as the issue was trading in the primary market, or the press maintained its interest and coverage. Once the secondary market was left to determine the *value level* at which such paper should trade, investors and market makers soon showed their true feelings — through the size of the discount and the width of the bid-offered spread! This effect was frequently compounded by extensive copying of successful, innovative, issues resulting in rapid saturation of limited investor demand.

Some of these issues were more than attempts to sell a product purchased in the *wholesale* market at a *retail price*, and investors quickly learned to be wary of conspicuously clever forms of financing. Many of the ideas backing these issues were sound (such as option linked FRNs, equity index linked bonds, dual currency bonds and bonds with embedded or discrete options). However, investors became unwilling to experiment with these instruments in their portfolios, even if the particular 'play' suited their portfolios, because they were unwilling to take both an immediate capital loss on market revaluation *and* be exposed to an illiquid security.

As many of the hedge techniques are now widely available, investors can create for themselves (or have made for them) instruments which have their desired performance characteristics without the need for a public issue, and more importantly, without the need for a lead manager to build significant risk premium into the pricing. This offers significant benefits for investors who are specific about their requirements and selective about their investment bankers.

Changes in the hedging products market

The interest rate swap market is now quite mature in US dollars, but still undeveloped in most other currencies (see Chapter 3 for a full analysis). The interest rate swap will continue to develop in other currencies as more market participants become familiar with transacting and accounting for them: this will lead to increased volume. One result of higher volume will be more swaps warehouses which will facilitate greater liquidity and narrower dealing spreads as competing swaps market makers become increasingly aggressive in their pricing.

Currency swaps

The currency swap market will continue to be a hybrid market which trades interest rate differentials between currencies. Inside banks it will continue to be located somewhere between the long-term foreign exchange desk and the interest rate swap warehouse. Its growth will be largely determined by the same factors which drive those markets; currency and interest rate volatility to stimulate demand combined with the spread of the technology which enables market participants to value, and hence use, swaps.

Options

The market for long-term money market interest rate options (caps, floors and combinations such as collars and corridors, against Libor) has grown steadily, but the market for long-term bond options remains embryonic. This is due to a combination of the mathematical complexities of pricing long-tenor bond options, as well as the cost and risks of hedging them. We remain optimistic that most of these problems can be overcome, in time, and that a long-term bond options market will become an integral part of the market in available hedge techniques.

Reserve requirements

Regulators will inevitably attempt to place a capital weighting on all banking transactions, irrespective of whether accountants treat them as balance sheet items or not. This represents a positive goal as banks should put capital against all types of risky transactions according to the amount of risk involved. Regulatory controls may be established to protect the weakest members of a market at the expense of the strongest and may be unable to distinguish between different qualities of risk in each risk category. Both of these shortcomings typically have the effect of forcing bankers to select more risky and more profitable transactions than they would do in the absence of regulation; this effect is the opposite to that desired by the regulators.

Another by-product of regulation is higher transation costs caused by allocating the cost of the capital required to be held against the transaction into its pricing. This reduces the efficiency of those markets whose efficiency is improved by widespread application of hedge techniques. However, pricing adjusted for cost of capital is preferable to pricing based on no risk just because the risk is not translated into balance sheet assets. Regulation is probabley inevitable and can be expected for the swaps and options markets in the near future. Regulation does at least have the advantage of ensuring a minimum form of prudential control across all market participants; if this is global as well as local it can be said to be a real achievement.[1]

The Future

Further development of the market in synthetic securities will occur both as the cost of executing swaps (especially currency swaps) falls and as new hedge techniques (in particular options) are brought to bear on restructuring investment instruments. However, the synthetic security is fundamentally an arbitrage between the bond market and the market for hedge techniques. For this reason, three independent factors determine the likely future amount of activity devoted to synthetic securities:

— increased volatility between the bond swap and options markets, making the opportunities to exploit the synthetics arbitrage more prevalent;

— further growth in the underlying bond and swap markets; or

— much wider understanding and use of the available hedge techniques by market participants in general, and investors in particular.

The amount of likely *future volatility* between markets is uncertain, but it is clear that the politicians and bureaucrats who are responsible for the management of the economic system will continue to propagate random change (however unknowingly) through their comments and actions.

The future *growth of the market* in securitised instruments, with which we are largely concerned here, will be determined by the extent and tightness of the controls imposed by financial market regulators on non-securitised instruments (ie on balance sheet bank lending) relative to securitised ones. Regulators, by their very nature, have no alternative but to follow along in the wake of market developments and attempt to clean up whatever mess is left behind after the bankers have moved on to pastures new. This causes regulators to be in the unenviable position of having to concentrate on the current crisis, knowing that by their action they cause bankers to innovate new, unregulated or less regulated, ways of doing business. For example, the less developed countries (LDC) debt crisis resulted in higher bank capital adequacy ratios worldwide, which accelerated the trend towards the less regulated global securitisation of debt.

[1] The Bank for International Settlements in a consultative paper published in December 1987 proposed the global introduction of such rules by 1992.

The *new hedge techniques* will become more broadly understood and this will result in widespread application both by market professionals and, more importantly, by investors.

As synthetic securities are fundamentally an arbitrage technique it is clear that the market cannot grow independently of the underlying markets in bonds or hedges. All pure arbitrages improve the efficiency of the underlying market, as we have shown with the behaviour of bonds in the secondary market (Chapter 8). As the bond markets now trade more closely to value than previously, arbitrage can only continue until the market efficiency improves to the point where the transaction costs of effecting the arbitrage are greater than the potential gain. (However, the Eurobond market with its multiplicity of issues and unique trading style is unlikely to become so efficient as to preclude arbitrage for some time.) These two points, size of the underlying market and cost of implementing an arbitrage transaction, also indicate which market professionals can be expected to be the major players in future. These must be those with a broad market presence — trading securities in the secondary market combined with the lowest transaction costs — for a full range of hedge techniques.

Conclusions

The market in synthetic instruments can be expected to grow as the underlying markets grow and financial hedge technology becomes better understood by a wider group of users. This growth, however, may be constrained by reduced volatility and higher transaction costs stemming from the effects of regulation.

Issuers will be less able to use structured transactions using the latest hedge techniques to generate arbitrage returns which lower their effective cost of raising funds, as investors will be equally able to value and transact these hedges.

Investors will increasingly disregard which types of paper are available in the market as they will decide exactly what it is they want from an investment and, if such an instrument does not exist, they will either make it themselvs or have it made for them.

Finally, the changing behaviour of investors will dominate the future development of the market in synthetic securities. If they have not done so already, investors should change their methods from evaluating all possible investment opportunities and purchasing those closest to their needs, to focusing upon their own specific requirements and arranging for instruments which fit these needs to be created. Both the technology and the expertise is available, and investors should not be afraid to use them.